THE BEING OF BUSINESS:
INTERVIEWS FROM
ARTISTS,
INTERIOR
DESIGNERS,
AND FOODIES
ON THEIR LIVES'
WORK

COMPILED BY ONNA CARR
OF THE MONDAY,
WEDNESDAY, AND FRIDAY
FINDS BLOG AT
THELITTLEGREENHOUSEONTHECORNER.COM

The Being of Business: Interviews from Artists, Interior Designers, and Foodies on Their Lives' Work

Compiled by Onna Carr of http://thelittlegreenhouseonthecorner.com

Thanks to my family, who suggested that I compile my blog's interviews into a book and who assisted by reading and editing this manuscript for publication.

Thanks to those featured in the following interviews, listed in order of appearance in this collection:

Alexandra Hilton, Lisa Chapman, Petra Hall, Gabriela Galbenus, Lydia Inglett, Melinda Dominico, Merissa A. Alink, Justin Rhodes, Selina Fowler, Arjuna Noor, April J. Harris, Jennifer Herwitt, Marie Burgos, Stephanie Jeffries, Kyrsten Attig, Kimberly C. Lyons, Patti Cowger, Jaqueline de Araujo, Jaqueline deMontravel, Laurence Carr, Gilly Craft, Sara Ho, Andrea Gramaccia, Davian Rhodes, Giulia Delpiano, Shelley Dozier-Mckee, Dina Caruso, Diana Deitrick, Sim Barker, Paddy Rasmussen, Nancy Iraggi, Heather Chase, Debbie Fred, Karista Bennett, and Karie Engels—you all made this book possible by sharing your life's work via your interviews. Thank you for sharing your stories and the "being" in your businesses!

Thank you for purchasing <u>The Being of Business: Interviews by Artists, Interior Designers, and Foodies on Their Lives' Work</u>. This book contains interviews that came from my website, <u>http://thelittlegreenhouseonthecorner.com</u>'s, blog, <u>http://www.thelittlegreenhouseonthecorner.com/blog</u>, Monday, Wednesday, Friday Finds Blog. In the spring of 2017, I decided have Monday, Wednesday, Friday Finds Blog branch out to include a series of interview posts which have featured artists, interior designers, and foodies from around the world. This book includes thirty-eight of these interviews. The people interviewed have been engaging and informative as they answer a few basic questions as to why they do what they do (the being of business for them) and what they have learned from their life's work. Those featured here were kind enough to share their knowledge with the readers of my blog and have thoughtfully agreed to be featured in this book so that others' may learn from their work.

These thirty-eight interviews have become a hub through which readers can have a virtual visit across the table with these very talented interviewed individuals that can be enjoyed in any place and in any kind of weather with the perfect cuppa. Thank you for being one of these readers.

Have a lovely day,

Onna Carr

December 3, 2018

Friday Finds:

The Artists

Alexandra Hilton of Bagel Face UK

April 21, 2017

By Alexandra Hilton with Onna Carr

This week, I am featuring an interview with Alexandra Hilton, the owner and founder of Bagel Face UK. Alexandra runs a wonderful Etsy shop,

https://www.etsy.com/shop/bagelfaceuk, where she sells her handcrafted, crocheted creations: booties, baby sets, blankets, garlands, cushions, and bookmarks. Bagel Face UK also has a beautiful and well-followed Instagram account, https://www.instagram.com/ bagelfaceuk/ and Facebook Page, https://www.facebook.com/bagelfaceuk, where Alexandra updates her followers about her newest projects and items for sale. Bagel Face UK specializes in Bespoke baby products crafted with care for little ones. I hope that you find Alexandra and her business, Bagel Face UK, as interesting and fun as I did.

What led you to start Bagel Face UK?

I first learned to crochet while studying textiles at college. I loved crocheting from the very beginning and used to crochet with anything I could find including fabric and fishing wire. During the summer between finishing college and starting university, I began crocheting tops and bikinis which sold really well on Depop. Obviously, once I started studying at university, I had a lot less

free time to crochet. I studied 3D design in university, specializing in interiors. Although I had a huge workload, it was mainly drawing and computer work, so I really missed being "hands-on." After graduating, I worked on a few freelance jobs and internships but eventually decided to "give it a shot" at running my own business full-time. Bagel Face UK has only officially been open since January of this year!

I love the name of your business! I am just curious how you arrived at "Bagel Face UK" for a name?

It was actually a family member that called me "Bagel" once on holiday years ago. Ever since then, the name stuck. I'm now referred to as "Bagel face," "Little bagel," or even "Bagel brain!" Bagel Face is pretty unique and catchy, so it just seemed like the perfect business name for me!

What is your favorite aspect of owning and operating Bagel Face UK?

I love every single aspect from designing new products, to picking out suitable yarns, to creating the products, and photographing the finished

creations! I especially love receiving photographs of little people wearing my booties! It's amazing to be able to work from home on my own time: I spend so much more time with my family now, and my work is even better when my business is something I really enjoy doing too.

What have you learned the most from opening and running your business?

I think the main thing is to learn how to manage your time wisely. It's very easy to underestimate how hard it is to run a business; you quickly realize there are not enough hours in a day! As I am a sole trader, I have to manage my accounts, my social media platforms, and my online selling platforms as well as sourcing materials and actually making the products, which is much more time consuming than one would think.

What tips and ideas do you have for others who would like to sell handcrafted items and/or to open an Etsy store?

Go for it! You have nothing to lose—even if you start off with something really small and simple. It costs nothing to register as a business, open a Paypal account and start up a Facebook page! A lot of small businesses start from hobbies, just make sure you choose to make and to sell something you have a real passion for and don't be afraid of a challenge. It's true what they say: choose a job you love and you will never have to work a day in your life.

What are your favorite items to craft for your business?

I'm really enjoying working on my range of baby shoes and booties at the moment, although I am looking forward to some warmer weather too so I can start creating some more beautiful bikinis!

What is at the heart of your business that you want your customers to take home?

Every single item that I make has been designed and made with love. I have always been a huge fan of handmade and unique one-off pieces. I'm proud to say that I contribute to the growing handmade industry. Buying from small businesses not only supports people like me so that we can do what we love to do, it ensures you get a truly unique and high quality item that you won't ever find on High Street.

Alexandra and her business, Bagel Face UK, can be followed on the platforms listed:

Etsy— https://www.etsy.com/shop/bagelfaceuk

Facebook Page—https://www.facebook.com/bagelfaceuk,

Instagram—https://www.instagram.com/ bagelfaceuk/

Photos courtesy of and with permission from Alexandra Hilton of Bagel Face UK.

Lisa Chapman of Randall Barbera

April 28, 2017

By Lisa Chapman with Onna Carr

This week, I am featuring an interview with Lisa Chapman, vice president and general Manager of Randall Barbera Antique Trunk Restoration and Design. Lisa's company restores antique trunks into beautiful works of art that will last for many years and provide elegance to the interiors that feature them. Their site, http://randallbarbera.com/, has an online store, gallery, and further information on their trunk restoration services.

What led you to Randall Barbera?

I started working with Randall in 2003. We were refinishing and crafting various pieces of furniture, mostly for people within our neighborhood at the time.

I am just curious why the business is named Randall Barbera?

Randall Barbera is the person who started this business, and when he launched his first website, that's the URL he used. Lots of designers use their name, and I guess he just followed suit.

What is your favorite aspect of working at Randall Barbera?

Since it is just he and I, I get involved in everything from working on restorations to designing and building custom trunks. He is very supportive and encouraging when it comes to creativity and this, among other things, makes for a great working environment. Being involved at the very start of a project, and seeing it evolve until completion is very satisfying. I've had some pretty crazy design ideas over the years and he has never nixed any of them!

What have you learned the most from Randall Barbera?

That anything is fixable. There are no such things as "mistakes," it's all just part of the evolutionary process. Sometimes I will be looking at a restoration job that comes through the door thinking, "Wow! This thing is BEYOND repair," but I've learned to think outside of the box and to realize that I might have to attempt a treatment that I'm inexperienced in and must not to be afraid to try. Randall always says that persistence will always win out in the long run.

What tips and ideas do you have for others who would like to start or to join a similar business specializing in antique restoration?

Find out as much as you can about an existing company. Look at their websites. See what their specialty is and then imagine if it were your business. What would you do to help the effort? What would you do differently? What could your skills add to the betterment of the product(s)? Somehow, try to get your hands on one of the products that they offer, or something similar. Take it apart and take careful notes on how it was put together. It seems as though most restoration companies are fairly small entities, and as such, your personality and your approach to your work should

be rooted in the same passion as they have. It's really hard work! Be careful what you wish for!!

What is one of your favorite products available at Randall Barbera?

We have a metal covered trunk which I redesigned by using a turquoise enamel on the exterior finish. I've always been a fan of retro, 1950-ish kitchen appliances, like stoves and refrigerators as I love the bright colors: they have a very basic, uncomplicated 'vibe' to them. I used a large black nail-head in the design too, and I stained and refinished the exterior wooden slats black. Randall loved the idea, and we've decided to produce more—in different colors. After all, shouldn't every kitchen have a trunk as an accent?!

What is at the heart of Randall Barbera that you want your customers to take home?

That's easy! QUALITY! We make sure that every piece that we restore or build is at the top of its game, and will last for the next few generations, at least. Whether we are working on a Louis Vuitton, or an old Army footlocker, we know that with every trunk, there is sentimental attachment. We appreciate that our clients put their trust in us, and we respect and value this trust by delivering back to them their precious antique in a condition that (we hope) will exceed their expectations.

Lisa and her company, Randall Barbera, can be followed on the platforms listed:

Facebook—https://www.facebook.com/RandallBarberaLtd

Instagram—https://www.instagram.com/randallbarberaantiquetrunks/

Linkedin—https://www.linkedin.com/in/randall-barbera-ba9632b/?trk=nav_responsive_tab_profile

Pinterest—https://www.pinterest.com/Mallatier/

Twitter—https://twitter.com/randallbarbera

Photos courtesy of and used with permission from Lisa Chapman of Randall Barbera.

Petra Hall of Petronella Hall

May 26, 2017

Onna Carr with Petra Hall

Petra Hall is the owner of Petronella Hall, a company specializing in wallpaper, fabric, cushions, and Bespoke products from the UK. Petra's interview is a fascinating look at her company and their beautiful line of elegant products.

What led you to start Petronella Hall?

I launched Petronella Hall fabrics in 2015, adding the wallpapers in 2016. I have always been in design of some sort since my A levels, though mainly fashion. At the age of forty-two, I finally enrolled in an art degree – illustration—it's been a long road to get here. I completed the degree, loved it, and went to work for a graphic design/marketing company—it definitely wasn't for me. Whilst at Uni, I used the print room to screen-print textiles for my home. The technician was so sweet, he would let me print meters of it on the students' days off and hang it all from the

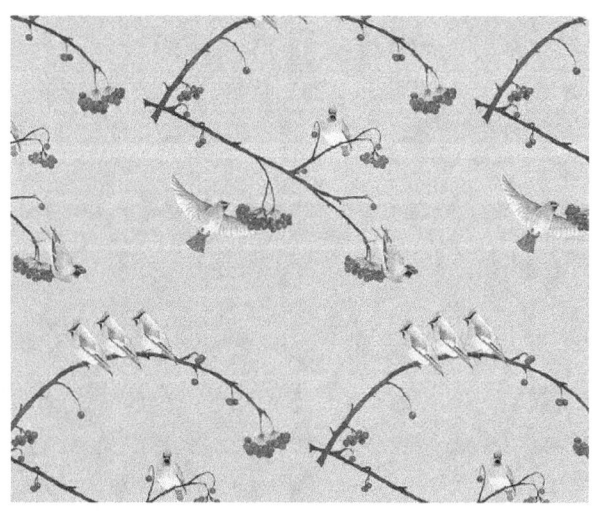

ceiling to dry. One weekend a friend popped over, saw my newly hung Dragonfly curtains and said "That's it! That's what you should do—design fabrics for the home!" It was one of those eureka moments, when the whole of your being says "YES! YES! YES!" So I excitedly began a steep learning curve. Ten months in, and through a friend of a friend, we met up with Stephen Lewis of Lewis and Wood, he looked at the designs and said "Put them on wallpaper, don't mess about – just get on with it," So we did.

I love the name of your business, and I am just curious how you arrived at "Petronella Hall" for a name?

Thank you. Actually, "Petronella" is my real name. I wrestled a long time with using it, it seemed so presumptuous. I was teased mercilessly at school about it. I've kept it quiet for a long time, but now, for this season, it seems to fit. It means "large rock," which is funny as I'm only 5'4"!

What is your favorite aspect of owning and managing Petronella Hall?

Seeing my own designs being used in other people's homes.

What have you learned the most from opening Petronella Hall?

Nothing is straightforward. Don't panic: you'll find a way.

What tips and ideas do you have for others who would like to start an interior design business?

Just get on and do it. It's never too late.

What are your favorite products of Petronella Hall?

Ha-ha, well I designed them – so all of them!

What is at the heart of Petronella Hall that you want your visitors to take home?

A love for the beauty of nature with a dose of fun!

Petra Hall and her company, Petronella Hall, can be followed on the platforms listed:

Facebook—https://www.facebook.com/Petronellafabrics

Instagram—https://www.instagram.com/petronella_hall_fabrics/

LinkedIn—https://www.linkedin.com/in/petra-hall-15a01326/

Pinterest—https://uk.pinterest.com/petronella66/

Twitter: https://twitter.com/Petronellahall

Photos courtesy of and used with permission from Petra Hall of Petronella Hall.

Gabriela Galbenus, Feng Shui Consultant

October 10, 2017

Gabriela Galbenus with Onna Carr

Gabriela Galbenus, founder of The London Feng Shui and former executive member of the Feng Shui Society, is featured in this week's interview post.

What led you to become a Feng Shui Consultant?

All my life I was amazed by the ancient civilizations how they were able, with no instruments, to develop complex understanding of astronomy, to build complex cities with no modern machinery, to communicate with one another with no written language, and to figure out how to grow crops even in the most inhospitable places. Scientists have tried for decades to understand how these civilizations have made such discoveries with limited technology. Looking at these ancient civilizations' advancements from a Feng Shui perspective, I believe they gained all the knowledge by observing and replaying nature. Since I was a child, I have believed in Feng Shui's principles without knowing about its existence until 10 years ago, when I come across Feng Shui, and from that day on, my journey of learning hasn't stopped.

What is your favorite aspect of being a Feng Shui Consultant?

There is not just one favorite aspect that I love about my job, but many. One aspect is the observation; I observe, question, and discover every time I come across a piece of land. The second favorite aspect is application; that is the Yang (active) side of my job, and I love every minute of it. Then, the client contact aspect; that is the most amazing experience for me. Being able to redirect and to revitalize people's energy is not easy, but it is the most rewarding experience that one can experience. And finally, research and learning; discovering ancient systems to calculate and gather the Qi flow from the environment.

What have you learned the most from your career in Feng Shui?

Trying always to do the important things, at the right time, at the right place, with the right people!

What tips and ideas do you have for others who would like to be Feng Shui Consultants?

Learning Feng Shui is about observing and understanding both your environment and yourself. Don't be scared of what you see, use common sense. Most importantly, always question the information you are learning. Each country has its own Feng Shui. However, Chinese Feng Shui scholars have done a great job on passing on useful information about how energy works. Although, Feng Shui has been lost in bad translations and misinterpretation, there remains so much material to still be learned.

What is at the heart of your career in Feng Shui that you want your clients to take home?

Understanding the environment! Feng Shui doesn't make miracles but uses what we have around us: the environment. We tap into Qi and make use of the energies surrounding us to foster a positive change in our health, our careers, our wealth, and our relationships.

Gabriela can be followed on the platforms listed:

Website: http://www.thelondonfengshui.co.uk

Facebook: http://www.facebook.com/thelondonfengshui

Guest speaker at the BBC Politics: http://www.youtube.com/watch?v=FcT7dcql0Xw

Lydia Inglett of http://starbookspublishing.com

October 27, 2017

By Lydia Inglett with Onna Carr

What led you to become a publisher?

Being a voracious reader combined with artistic creativity and a desire to do good work.

What is your favorite aspect of being a publisher?

Working with authors, artists, and photographers to develop words and images into a beautiful experience for the reader. I dream and think in books!

What have you learned the most from your career as a publisher?

It is a challenging business. The cultural myth is that the publisher is the heavy, which is not the case: the publisher takes the all the risk.

What tips and ideas do you have for others who would like to become publishers?

Never forget the reader and make the book cover draw them from across the room.

What are your favorite features of being a publisher?

Receiving the advance copies of a new book.

What is at the heart of your career in publishing that you want your clients to take home?

A publisher who is at once commercially-minded and sensitive to the content and to the vision of the author, the artist, or the photographer.

Lydia and http://www.starbooks.com can be followed on the platforms listed:

Facebook—https://www.facebook.com/Starbooksbiz

Instagram—https://www.instagram.com/starbooks.biz/

Pinterest—https://www.pinterest.com/starbooksbiz/starbooksbiz/

Twitter—https://www.twitter.com/LydiaPubs

Websites—https://www.starbooks.biz and http://www.lydiainglett.com

Photo courtesy of and used with permission from Lydia Inglett.

Snapshots are Just Moments in Time: Remembering Today . . . Tomorrow—an Interview with Melinda Dominico

March 9, 2018

Melinda Dominico with Onna Carr

What led you to become a photographer?

My love for photography and interior design came to me early. Using our family's home as a drawing board, my doodles were always of homes: I would design the interiors— forever rearranging the furniture. This was helpful when I began working in Property Management as a Leasing Consultant in Dallas, Texas, and in the Washington DC Metro area. My job description constantly included decorating model apartments, taking pictures to create albums and videos of each property inside and out, creating ads for apartment finder books, designing and sending out flyers (pre-social media), and to sell, sell, sell. I was consistently in top sales in both locations. Furthermore, I co-created "The Apartment Locator Service" for Southern Management Corporation for David Hillman in the Washington DC Metro area in the 80's, which is still thriving strong today.

Not long after that, I married, and we had two children. Because my husband traveled extensively for work, I was fortunate to have the option of staying at home, which

is where I took the opportunity to become involved with the schools and with our community.   Again, I usually had something to do with cameras and video, so I embraced it.

When I first decided to be a photographer it was difficult because I didn't have the skills or the opportunities for a higher education, so I learned on the job by throwing myself into the thick of it. At this point, the only thing I knew was how to take a normal picture and what I liked taking pictures of. Our children were young and in sports, so I began taking pictures from the stands, then from around the perimeter, finally progressing onto the field even obtaining a press pass from the local high school. At the same time, I ordered every photography book on the topics I was interested in along with learning how to build websites and to meet the demands of social media. I spent a lot of time in trial and error—only progressing forward a little at a time. I did a lot of pro-bono work which was just a way for me to learn something new, which I did each time I had a new project.

My dream has been to travel everywhere, taking pictures that I can in turn sell as my art work. 20/20 hindsight showed me the many times in my past I had been given opportunities which included photography, videography and decorating in some way. I realized what I had created and accomplished for so many I now had the courage and chance to do for myself.

I opened the doors of my photography business in 2005 but it wasn't until 2016 when I created PhotoDesigns for Interior Designs that things really started to take off. Among offering my natural landscape photo-journalistic images, I began to create unique drawing-like artwork from selected photo image pieces. I wanted to bring interior space to life with my

numerous themes for homes, offices, hotels, restaurants, staging homes, and more—to match any decor or atmosphere. My goal is to "Un-Norm Your Walls."

The changes have been extreme from 2005 to 2018. I now have a social presence on Facebook, LinkedIn, Zazzle, Fine Art America, Pinterest, and Twitter along with my own website http://www.DominicoPhotography.com. This past year, I was featured in a Pittsburgh fashion magazine, *PGH Avenue West*. I also display and sell my artwork at a well-known chic art gallery, the Appalachian Creativity Center, in Connellsville, PA, as well as in Rostraver, PA, at the newly opened Village Lane Shoppes, which offers antiques and more. My biggest business accomplishment came in the summer of 2017 when I won the "Close To Home" contest with The Bon-Ton Department store. They have an area within their stores dedicated to selling locally-made products from local artists along with online sells. Bon-Ton has given me an incredible opportunity to be seen by so many more potential clients. In addition, I sell several pieces of my collections on two online stores, Fine Art America and Zazzle. Both allow me to incorporate my PhotoDesigns on a vast array of merchandise to sell directly to the public via the internet. They allow me to customize and to create decor to tailor to any space in its entirety. Not just frames or canvas anymore: I can do shower curtains, beach towels, door mats, glassware, place mats, mugs, clocks, lampshades, blankets, pillows—you name it, and I can probably customize it for you!

What is your favorite aspect of being a photographer?

I choose what I want to take pictures of plus I truly take pleasure interacting with so many different people. Most of all, I enjoy creating one-of-a-kind designs with the photographs I take: each one is unique unto itself. Most fun for me is taking pictures out of the passenger window while my husband drives us all over our amazing country. I love doing this because I never know what I'm going to get until I view it later: kind of like a box of chocolates. In addition, this method has helped me to get better at my on-the-fly timing.

What have you learned the most from your career in photography?

The true meaning of starving artist! You'd better have a good sense of humor and another source of income when you start out. Don't compare yourself to other photographers—be yourself. In addition, you will find many who feel the need to give their opinion with the heightened need to criticize, especially when they find out you haven't been "formally educated." As with anything else in life, not everyone will like everything you do. Period. It's your calling—not theirs.

What tips and ideas do you have for others who would like to be photographers?

For me, when I look at art, it's about how it makes me feel, not that it was taken at a particular aperture or lens or if it was or wasn't on a tri-pod. I'm imperfect and so are my PhotoDesigns: that's what makes them so incredibly unique! Be true to yourself! Create your own opportunities: they don't all just fall into our laps. NEVER give up! NEVER allow anyone to tell you that you need a formal education to become who you are to live your dream! Sure the road is bumpy and sure there are times we must climb. Sometimes we must fall, and yes, sometimes we must fail in order to succeed. Sometimes the meaning of our success doesn't come quick enough. Sometimes we can't see our successes until we look back. But, is it worth it? YES! ALWAYS BELIEVE in yourself! Remember one way or another we're all in the same boat: you're not alone. Define your own path, push forward! Carry on!

What are your favorite features of being a photographer?

The world IS my office so I have no constraints. Beauty is all around us, and I feel compelled to capture as much as I possibly can by carrying my camera with me just for the fact I can't recreate the moments that have passed. My photos are about catching life as it happens in front of me: a journey with me—as seen by me. My photos are a point in time that can never be recaptured or even repeated. I take pleasure in creating distinctive, special, and meaningful pieces.

What is at the heart of your career in photography that you want your clients to take home?

When my clients look at their photos or PhotoDesigns, I want them to be taken there: I want them to remember today tomorrow regardless of whether or not it's senior pictures, weddings, or my unconventional landscape PhotoDesigns. Since quality photos are an investment, I go above and beyond what the client expects—always trying to go the extra mile most times with them not even realizing it.

Melinda Dominico can be followed on the platforms listed:

Facebook--http://www.facebook.com/DominicoPhotography

Fine Art America-- https://fineartamerica.com/artists/melinda+dominico/photographs

Pinterest-- https://www.pinterest.com/dominicophotog/?eq=dominico%20photo&etslf=10320

Twitter--https://twitter.com/MelindaDominico

Website--http://www.DominicoPhotography.com

Zazzle--https://www.zazzle.com/dominicophotography

All Photos courtesy of and used with permission from Melinda Dominico.

Merissa A. Alink of
http://www.littlehouseliving.com

April 6, 2018

Merissa A. Alink with Onna Carr

What led you to start
http://littlehouseliving.com?

I started Little House Living in 2009 after wanting to share my husband and I's journey through frugal living. We were newly married and had already survived through everything from unemployment to living in a camper. We pulled ourselves up by our bootstraps, and I wanted to share how anyone can make the most with what they have.

What is your favorite aspect of http://littlehouseliving.com?

I love being able to share my story and to offer encouragement to those who are in a similar walk of life.

What have you learned the most from http://littlehouseliving.com?

Over the past nine years of blogging, I have learned how to have a thicker skin. I had no idea what people will say when they are hiding behind a computer screen! At times, things have been difficult, but I know what my mission is and for every naysayer there are a thousand others who will find the advice helpful.

What tips and ideas do you have for others who would like to start a similar website and blog?

Be prepared to spend more time than you think you will need. I've discovered that actual writing is only about 20% of what I need to do to keep Little House Living running. Answering emails, working on social media, networking, and more all take a majority of my "work" time.

What are your favorite features of http://littlehouseliving.com?

I love that we have a wonderful community. There are so many helpful comments that come in each day, and our new Facebook group has been a wonderful extension of the blog readers!

Can you tell us a bit about your book, <u>Little House Living</u>?

My book is a wonderful collection of so many of my favorite things that I have made over the years of learning how to make the most with what I have. In the book, you will find recipes for household products, body and beauty items with very simple ingredients, recipes for my favorite pantry mixes and spices, and SO many frugal tips! Many people that have bought the book told me that it's their go-to book. Honestly it's my go-to book as well! *You can get Merrissa's amazing book via this link,* http://amzn.to/2Heg7Eb.

What is at the heart of http://littlehouseliving.com that you want your visitors to take home?

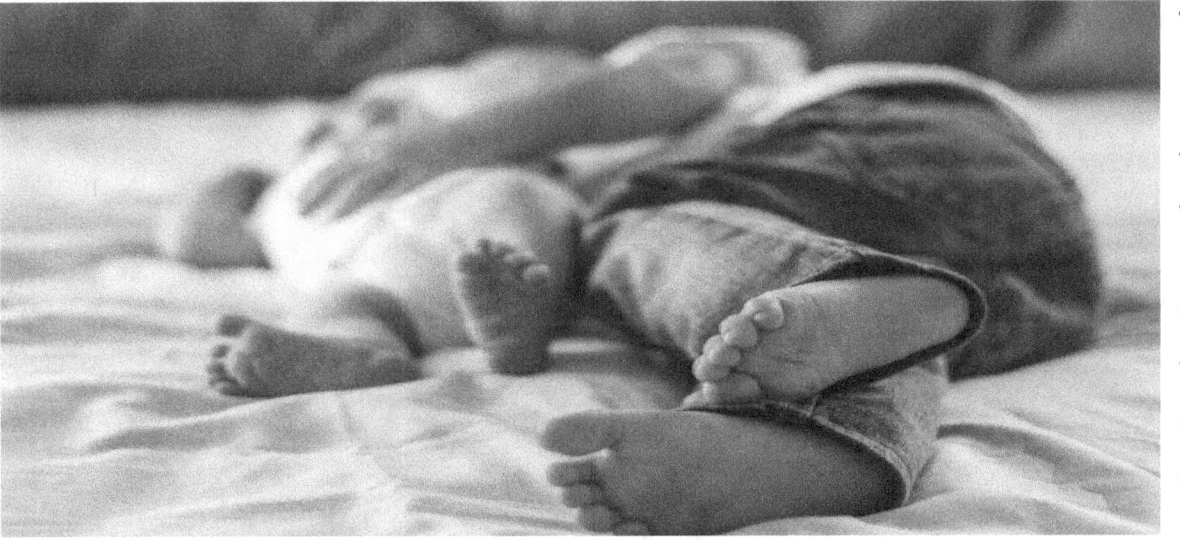

I hope that those who visit Little House Living will leave feeling encouraged and know that they can always come back for more. I'm the only one behind the scenes of Little House Living, so I will always be the one to answer the comments and emails that come in. If you are struggling with where you are at in life—maybe you are hoping to live a simpler life and things just feel so chaotic or perhaps you are trying to raise a family on a low, single income budget—wherever you are at in life, I hope that you will find encouragement and tips on Little House Living.

Merissa can be followed on the platforms listed:

Facebook: http://facebook.com/littlehouseliving

Instagram: http://instagram.com/littlehouseliving

Pinterest: http://pinterest.com/merissa_alink

Website: http://www.littlehouseliving.com

Twitter: http://twitter.com/lhliving

Youtube: https://www.youtube.com/user/littlehouseliving

Photo 1 courtesy of Priscilla Dupreeez on Unsplash, photo 2 courtesy of Pablo Heimplatz on Unsplash, and photo 3 courtesy of Isaac Deltoro on Unsplash.

**Justin Rhodes of
http://www.Abundantpermaculture.com
and the Justin Rhodes YouTube Channel**

April 13, 2018

Justin Rhodes with Onna Carr

**What led you to
start http://www.abundantpermaculture.com and your YouTube channel, Justin
Rhodes?**

A desire to run a family friendly business that helps folks grow more of their own food.

**What is your favorite aspect of www.abundantpermaculture.com and your
YouTube channel, Justin Rhodes?**

I actually love the creative process of creating a short film with my family.

**What have you learned the most
from http://www.abundantpermaculture.com and your YouTube channel, Justin
Rhodes?**

I've learned that business is certainly one of the #1 tools to reach a broad audience and to have the collective power of the individuals coming together to make a big, positive difference in the world.

What tips and ideas do you have for others who would like to have a similar life's work in permaculture and homesteading?

I'd say teach whatever you know, via your favorite platform (blog, VLOG, instructional video, podcast).

Essentially, produce quality content (continually getting better) and get it out there consistently. Then, be patient as your audience builds over time.

What are your favorite features of http://www.abundantpermaculture.com and your YouTube channel, Justin Rhodes?

As a creator of films, I LOVE that I don't have to go through anyone else to reach an audience. With the power of the internet anyone with an internet connection and a computer and/or camera can create their own channels!

Can you tell us a bit about your latest project, the Great America Farm Tour?

My family and I just returned from an epic road trip to all 50 states of America. Our goal was to highlight and to discover the greatest farms in America. I'm now wrapping up the edit on a documentary of the adventure. This documentary will release world-wide in a free premier viewing April 14th - 16th. Here are details on how to watch the free

premiere, https://abundantpermaculture.lpages.co/the-great-american-farm-tour-world-wide-premiere-2018/

What is at the heart of www.abundantpermaculture.com and your YouTube channel, Justin Rhodes?

 The desire to make the world a better place.

Justin and his family can be followed on the platforms listed:

Facebook—https://www.facebook.com/abundantpermaculturefarm/

Instagram--https://www.instagram.com/abundantpermaculture/?hl=en

Website--http://www.abundantpermaculture.com

YouTube—https://www.youtube.com/channel/UCOSGEokQQcdAVFuL_Aq8dlg

Photo 1 courtesy of Daigallelaby on Unsplash, photo 2 courtesy of Alexander Wang on Unsplash, photo 3 courtesy of Christian Joudrey on Unsplash, and photo 4 courtesy of Marcus Spiske on Unsplash.

Selina Fowler of CoeLux Srl

April 27, 2018

Selina Fowler with Onna Carr

What led you to pursue your career in the high-tech industry with CoeLux Srl?

I started career within retail design back in 2002, when I was a mere 22 years old! My first position was working as a project manager within Vitrashop. I learned all about shop-fitting: what trades are involved and how to take the design from concept with designers/architects/ retailers through to completion. It was a very steep learning curve, and I remember vividly taking home the product manuals and reading them each night to understand what I was working with! My father helped me understand reading drawings as he was a ductwork engineer and has extensive knowledge of working with trades and following plans. My next move was where I really started my lighting career. I joined a company called Microlights, as a retail lighting specialist: it was here where John Chamberlin taught me my basic lighting knowledge. Learning about all the various lamp types, how they emit light and how we see that light through to how a product is manufactured and how it controls light output. How we use these tools to create a look and feel of an environment—creating brand identity. I loved this job, and I love the creativity of designing with light.

I was approached by CoeLux as it just so happens that I was aware of the product and had actually introduced it to one of my retail clients as a possible solution in their lighting design. I loved the product, and I could see its potential to change the way we light interiors, so I was very open to a discussion. I met with Paolo Di Trapani and was infused with his passion and with his belief in the technology. I started my role with CoeLux as Head of UK Projects at the end of March 2017.

What is your favorite aspect of CoeLux Srl?

CoeLux has an amazing technology and a passion to create products which enhance the perception of natural light. The process within the product is truly unique. Paolo Di Trapani, our founder, is a professor, and he has spent over a decade creating experiments to study and to test how natural light works and it was this testing that led him to create our products. He is now pursuing independent studies to show the extent of the positive effects of this truly inspiring technology, on us the occupants (and on plants)!

What have you learned the most from CoeLux Srl?

Wow, I have learnt a lot in my short ten months within the position! Understanding the technology and how it works was the first task. With my background in lighting, this step wasn't too challenging for me. I also believe my mind is truly logical and having mathematical explanations helps me to understand quickly.

I work in the UK and have responsibility to increase awareness of the product. Although I have been involved in marketing before, taking sole responsibility for the UK has been a learning curve which I have enjoyed! I have taken part in trade shows, put on a round table event, entered and won a trade award, gained certification on a CPD as well as building relationships with large global companies.

I am also learning more about the effects of lighting and how it affects our biology. CoeLux is focused on bringing not only a beautiful product to market, but to truly enhance our environment and our lives. The product gives an emotive response that is hard to explain. I try to convey this in many ways, but a simplistic way would

be to ask someone how they feel when they open their curtains in the morning. To be greeted by a sunny day with a bright blue sky, most of us feel up-lifted and to have better days: this is what CoeLux does—it provides a positive lift in our moods. Learning about how this works and the biological and physiological responses in our bodies and plants is fascinating, and I love to learn.

What tips and ideas do you have for others who would like to pursue a similar career path in the high-tech industry?

Work for a company that creates something you are passionate about and that you understand. Be prepared to research and to continually learn. A thirst for knowledge is a key quality to working in a high-paced tech career.

What is at the heart of CoeLux Srl that you want your customers to take home?

That we believe in a better way of lighting. Creating human-centric products and biophilic designs that aid our built environment and create better spaces for us to live and to work in. If this approach were adopted by all there would be less depression, less workplace illness and better performance.

Selina can be followed on the platforms listed:

Facebook—http://www.facebook.com/coelux

Instagram—https://www.instagram.com/coelux/

LinkedIn— http://www.linkedin.com/in/selina-fowler-8a33b529

Website—http://www.coelux.com

Youtube—https://www.youtube.com/channel/UC1Z1lzD2sVPQgv51p98-93A

Photo 1 courtesy of Bruno Nascimento on Unsplash, photo 2 courtesy of Antonarillothe on Unsplash, and photo 4 courtesy of Kristin E. Willert on Unsplash.

Arjuna Noor of MOODSPACE

May 11, 2018

Arjuna Noor with Onna Carr

What led you to start MOODSPACE?

Recognizing the need to create iconic art experiences for hotels and hospitality on a grand scale: most art for corporations and hospitality institutions are low impact aesthetics and not a "memorable and iconic art experience." Rather than look at art as "pretty," I decided to look art as a "solution."

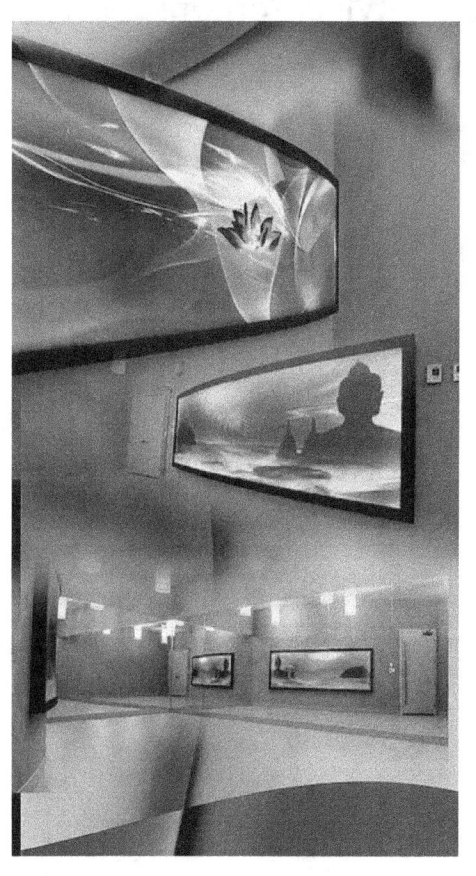

What is your favorite aspect of MOODSPACE?

To create visual magic for the thousands of people who will view the art every day in public institutions; Unlike art for private collectors, my art is viewed by over 10,000 people every day in the over 40 large scale iconic installations scattered throughout US, Canada, and the UK. That is very gratifying and serves larger purposes.

What have you learned the most from MOODSPACE?

 To have fun, to be dynamic, and to be relentlessly creative in art-making. I have learned to create beauty within constraints of building codes, design limitations, etc. I have learned in order to create meaningful large-scale art fusion of two concepts, art and commerce –art and technology to enable a meaningful experience.

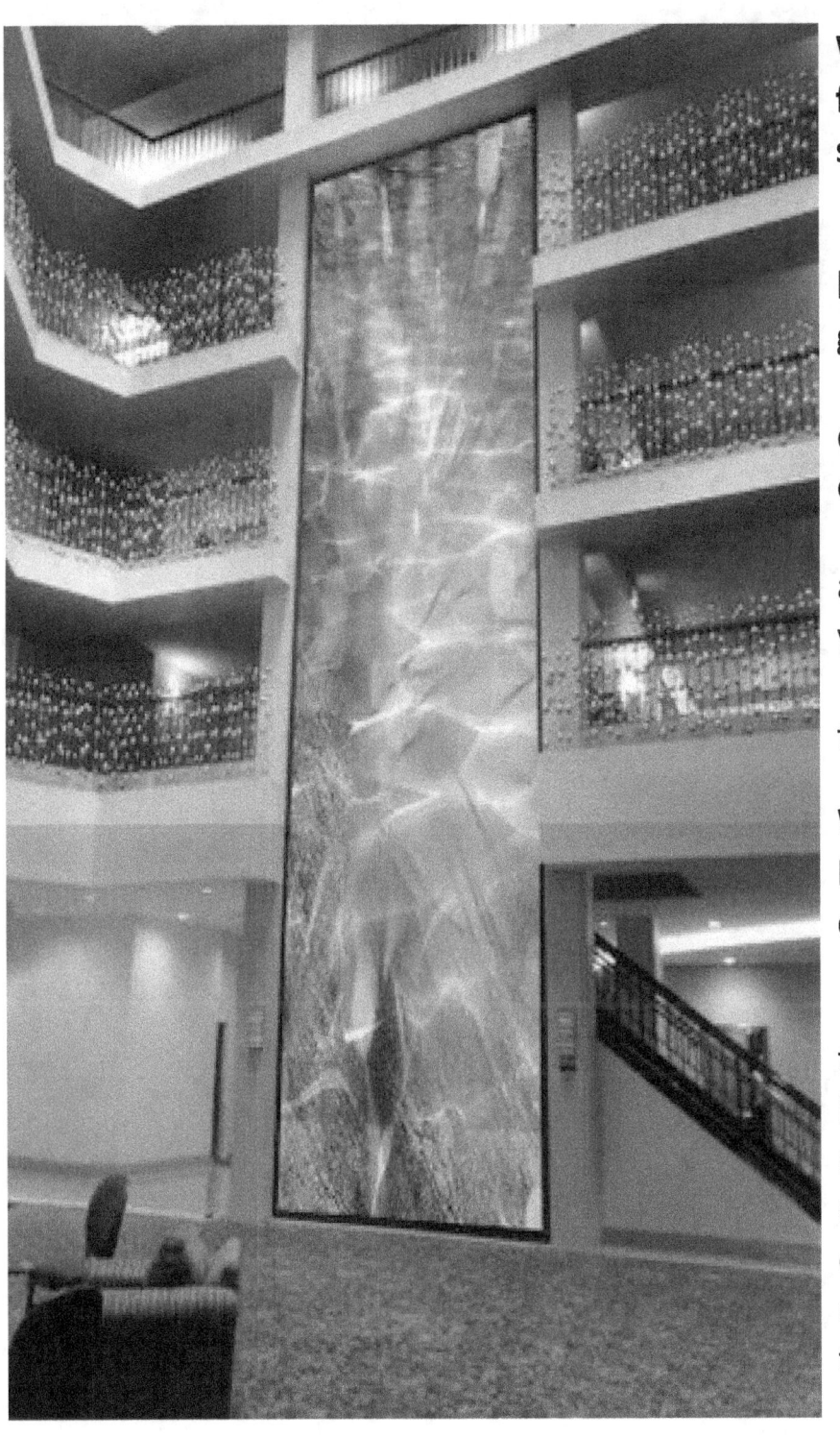

What tips and ideas do you have for others who would like to start a similar business?

- Conceptually sketch out a big picture roadmap with desired goals from the get-go.
- Update this "living" document regularly as the vision evolves.
- The most important thing about business is to insure that you are enjoying what you do.
- Avoid hiring employees till the entire work flow is down pat.

What is at the heart of MOODSPACE that you want your customers to take home?

A "feeling – an inspiration. Art transforms perception and imbues space with emotion. I am most fulfilled when a viewer is moved by my art, its core emotion and the universally unifying principles of humanity— that is beauty.

Arjuna can be followed on the platforms listed:

LinkedIn— https://www.linkedin.com/in/arjuna-noor-a1317614/

Facebook— https://www.facebook.com/arjuna.noor

Twitter— https://twitter.com/moodspace?lang=en

Website: http://www.moodspace.com

Email: arjuna@moodspace.com

All images courtesy of and used with permission from Arjuna Noor.

Petra Hall of Petronella Hall: a Return Visit :)

September 5, 2018

Petra Hall with Onna Carr

Last year, in May, Petra Hall of Petronella Hall was featured on this blog, and she has graciously returned this year to share some further insights into her business and some photos of her beautiful new line of nature-inspired wallpaper and fabrics.

What led you to begin your journey to become a textile and wallpaper designer and to open Petronella Hall?

I've played with fabrics since I made my first teddy's jacket at four- years-old. I finally went to Uni in my early 40's to do illustration, whilst there I screen-printed bedroom curtains with dragonflies for our home. After graduating, I worked briefly for a graphic design company, but I missed the fabrics too much. A good friend who's a product designer with a big interest in interiors saw my curtains and suggested I

illustrate on fabric, and I began Petronella Hall four years ago.

What is your favorite aspect of Petronella Hall?

My favourite aspect of course is the idea generation: drawing and development stage of a collection—that's the fun bit, you often don't know quite where it's going, and then it just unfolds before you: it gives me such a buzz!

What have you learned the most from being a textiles and wallpaper designer and from opening Petronella Hall?

In business things don't go according to plan but that's not the end of the world. Trust your instincts: they are usually right. Push every door—you never know what doors will open.

What tips and ideas do you have for others who are interested in pursuing a career in textile and wallpaper design?

You're never too old—go for it! Start small and grow as fast as your capacity grows.

What is at the heart of Petronella Hall that you want your customers to take home?

Nature is stunningly beautiful. I want to reflect some of that beauty in our homes.

Petra Hall and her company, Petronella Hall, can be followed on the platforms listed:

Facebook—https://www.facebook.com/Petronellafabrics/

Instagram—https://www.instagram.com/petronella_hall_fabrics/

Pinterest—https://www.pinterest.com/petronella66/

Twitter—https://twitter.com/petronellahall?lang=en

Website—http://www.petronellahall.com

All photos courtesy of and used with permission from Petra Hall of Petronella Hall.

April J Harris of
http://Apriljharris.com

September 7, 2018

April J. Harris with Onna Carr

What led you to become a writer, recipe developer, and blogger?

I have been a writer since I was very young, and I have continued to write after I married and had a son in 1993. I found myself writing more and more about what it was like to be a housewife and a stay-at-home mom, particularly in view of the way these roles were being perceived by society and the press. My husband suggested I collect the articles into a website (this was back before blogs even existed) and so, http://the21stcenturyhousewife.com was launched back in 2002. It featured a collection of essays to encourage other housewives and stay-at-home moms like me.

As blogging developed into a "thing," my readers began to get in touch, asking for more, so the blog was developed. After a couple of years, I added a "recipe of the week" feature, and from there http://the21stcenturyhousewife.com evolved into a lifestyle website with a heavy emphasis on food and travel. Then in 2014, as the new century became old news, I decided to rebrand and write under my own name, April J Harris. The blog was redesigned and relaunched as http://www.AprilJHarris.com.

What is your favorite aspect of being a writer, recipe developer, and a blogger?

I love that it allows me to continue to fulfill my role as a housewife whilst still travelling extensively and living our lives to the full. I can't devote as much time to it as I would like to, but I enjoy what I do!

What have you learned the most from being a writer, recipe developer, and blogger?

I've learned how important it is to create community and to reach out into the world. There is something so wonderful about connecting with your readers, and seeing them connect with each other. It makes me happy when people say they have made a recipe from my site, and it has become a family favorite that they have visited somewhere I have recommended and loved it or that I've helped them in some way.

What tips and ideas do you have for others who would like to be writers, recipe developers, and bloggers?

Don't be afraid to fail. I've learned so much from any mistakes I have made, and they have almost always led to better things. Just do what you love. Start the blog, write the book, and experiment in the kitchen. If it brings you pleasure, it's already a success on one level. If you can get your work out into the world and people enjoy it, then, so much the better.

What are your favorite features of being a writer, recipe developer, & blogger?

I'm able to be creative regardless of where I am. Obviously I need a kitchen to create recipes, but if I have my computer with me, I can write, edit photographs, and indulge my creativity absolutely anywhere. I also love that it has really expanded my horizons, allowing me to meet and to connect with other bloggers, learn new things and to have experiences I might not otherwise have had.

What is at the heart of being a writer, recipe developer, & blogger that you want your readers to take home?

For me, it's the ability to reach and to affect other people and to hopefully to benefit them. We are all here to help one another. I love what I do, and if something that brings me joy can be a help to someone else, so much the better! I want to encourage my readers to try new things, look at things through fresh eyes and do things differently. Life is an adventure, and if you only live it in your comfort zone, you are bound to miss out on some amazing experiences.

April can be followed on the platforms listed:

Facebook--https://www.facebook.com/The21stCenturyHousewife/

Instagram--https://www.instagram.com/apriljharris/

Pinterest--https://www.pinterest.co.uk/apriljharris/

Twitter--https://twitter.com/apriljharris

Website: http://www.Apriljharris.com

Photos courtesy of and used with permission from April J. Harris and Tara Taylor of Tara Taylor Photography.

Jennifer Herwitt of Jherwitt Jewelry

September 10, 2018

Jennifer Herwitt with Onna Carr

What led you to start Jherwitt?

Jherwitt was launched by Vogue. I have collected insects since I was a little girl. I would make my grammar school friends wear butterfly hats that I made, and we would forage through the forest for hours on end. I LOVED making dioramas for them to live in. I volunteered at the Bronx Zoo, helping to create the natural habitats for the live animals and for the taxidermy still life's.

I started Jherwitt "A Collection of Living Jewels" as my ode to the insect world. Each specimen you collect comes with a specimen box, a collection tag, and beautiful informational cards that inform you of the ecological and spiritual significance of insects in general, and for the specific insect you are collecting. The collection tags advise on how you are impacted by these diminutive wonders and how your life would be affected without them.

The same goes for the gems. For example, did you know that the softest element in the universe and the hardest element in the universe have the EXACT same chemical composition? Yes, lead in a pencil (the softest element) and a diamond (the hardest)

are composed of exactly the same elements! You can read my informational card for the incredible facts behind this wonder. They also explain how and why this happens. You will learn how the colors of diamonds come to be and the spiritual meaning the colors represent.

What is your favorite aspect of Jherwitt?

The incredibly beautiful and complex world of insects is my favorite aspect. Insects are often demonized, feared, and hated.

We only see the tip of the iceberg when it comes to knowing how many insects exist on this planet. Millions of insects remain undiscovered. Their contributions are often unknown, but they impact our lives in the most incredible ways. They are the garbage disposals of the world. Many forms of food would not exist without their pollination. Insects' power to heal and to feed the world goes unchecked. They teach us lessons in community, family, and rebirth and are beautiful beyond measure.

What have you learned the most from Jherwitt? That the world is a complex universe. Every living thing, animal, and plant has a purpose. We all affect one another. There is much to learn and admire from these diminutive wonders. Insecta

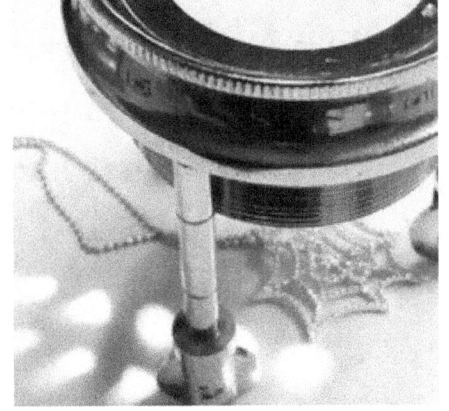

is the only class of animals that has adapted to every climate and topographical condition, from the glaciers of the far north to the boiling temperatures of hot springs. One square mile of rural land yields more insects than the number of people in the world, with an estimated 30 million species yet to be discovered. Adept at survival, some insects can go years without eating, while others

use warning colors or toxins to deter predators. Insects are often demonized for crop destruction; but, in reality, many plants depend on insects for pollination and the production of seeds. Without insects, at least 85% of flowering plants would not be able to reproduce. Critical sources of food such as strawberries, apples, kale, and squash would be lost as would much more of our biodiversity and many of our medicinal remedies.

Insects provide invaluable guidance in times of change, in matters of community, and in finding inspiration in the simplest purposes. From metamorphosis, we learn that change is essential for growth and that to achieve the new we must relinquish the old. Many insects live in colonies and play specific roles within their communities, instructing us in working and living as part of a group, and in finding value in our own individual purpose. Insects are attuned to the subtle signals of other insects as we too must be attuned to the subtle signals of life around us.

What tips and ideas do you have for others who would like to start a jewelry business?

For me, it is a labor of love. Dive in, be creative, use conflict-free gems and create supportive, safe jewels: making the world a better, more beautiful and loving place. Never negate the impact you have on this fragile planet. Do not take for granted that what you take from this planet has an effect. Be educated and be sure that what you use creates jobs and life and NEVER causes harm, extinction, or wars to obtain it. Conflict-free diamonds may cost more, but they insure a safe and ethical way to create an industry that celebrates what diamonds represent.

What are your favorite features of Jherwitt?

It's not just jewelry; it's a "Collection of Living Jewels."

What is at the heart of Jherwitt that you want your customers to take home?

The heart of Jherwitt is that I am an interior designer, multiple Emmy-award-winning set decorator, closet entomologist, and spinner of jewels. A native of New Jersey, I migrated from the East Coast to Los Angeles, where I transform personal living spaces and weave sets for film and television. All of my work is characterized by productive creativity and an unchecked enthusiasm for all things creeping and crawling. Inspired by the profound beauty and complexity of the insect world, I channel my love of insects into jeweled editions of these diminutive wonders, and I am sure to never overlook the positive omen of an anthill by my door.

Jennifer and her jewelry line, Jherwitt, were featured in Inspired by Insects, available through Amazon.com, https://www.amazon.com/Inspired-Insects-Bugs-Contemporary-Art/dp/0764353063

Jennifer and her jewelry company, Jherwitt, can be followed on the platforms listed:

Etsy—https://www.etsy.com/shop/JHerwittLivingJewels

Facebook—https://www.facebook.com/herwitt

Facebook Page—https://www.facebook.com/JHerwitt-304095069626047/ and https://www.facebook.com/Jherwitt/

Instagram—https://www.instagram.com/jherwitt_jewels/?hl=en and https://www.instagram.com/jenniferherwitt/?hl=en

Jewelstreet—https://www.jewelstreet.com/collections/Jherwitt

LinkedIn—https://www.linkedin.com/in/jennifer-herwitt-15a819b/

Lyst—https://www.lyst.com/designer/jherwitt/

Moddlinc—http://moddlinc.com/jennifer-herwitt/

Pink Lion—https://www.pinklion.com/shops/365-jherwitt

Onna Carr: US and Canadian Representative for LuXury Crystal Ireland

September 21, 2018

Onna Carr

What led you to become the US and Canadian representative for LuXury Crystal Ireland?

I have always appreciated fine crystal. I remember as a small child watching a film on touring Ireland, and I was mesmerized by the blowing and by the hand-cutting of crystal by Irish craftsmen in Waterford City. To be able to create objects of such beauty out of molten glass, which is formed into crystal, continues to amaze me to this day. When Noel Finan, the owner and founder of LuXury Crystal Ireland, asked me to be the company's US and Canadian representative, the opportunity seemed a serendipitous and natural progression as well as an exciting opportunity, and continues to remain so!

What is your favorite aspect of being the US and Canadian representative for LuXury Crystal Ireland?

I love that I am representing a rare breed of incredibly gifted master craftsmen whose art form goes back several hundred years and who are third and fourth generational craftsmen. The Irish team of generational craftsmen at LuXury Crystal Ireland is the only rare quality crystal manufacturer in the world today. These artisans create crystal as it should be made: a 33% full-lead, hand-cut, and hand-polished bespoke creation of the rarest and the purest quality in the world.

What have you learned the most from being a US and Canadian representative for LuXury Crystal Ireland?

That the unparalleled skill of Irish craftsmen is only one part of the story. There is also the uncanny power of those craftsmen to impart something magical to the finished crystal that the rest of Europe couldn't and still cannot replicate. I enjoy explaining our company and our legacy to customers via our promotional video, our catalogue, our book brochure, and samples of our crystal. I love talking to our customers about how LuXury Crystal Ireland's crystal truly is one-of-a-kind because, for more than 300 years, the Irish crystal craftsmen have been crafting the rarest and the purest crystal that, thanks to LuXury Crystal, remains available for today's generation to purchase and to pass on to their family.

What tips and ideas do you have for others who would like to represent a company and their product line?

Find a product that is different, bespoke, so that you have something unique and specialized to give yourself an edge of exclusivity in your business model. Learn as much as you can, not only about the company you wish to represent and their product line(s); but also, create strong interpersonal and professional webs that connect you and your product line(s) with a wide variety of other artisans and designers from all walks of life who help you to think about your work from different perspectives. By retaining and curating a sense of curiosity and being a life-long learner, you can open doors in unexpected and profitable ways that create a unique synchronicity in your journey.

What are your favorite features of being the US and Canadian Representative for LuXury Crystal Ireland?

That I get to introduce both US and Canadian buyers to the rarest and the purest quality crystal in the world—what an incredible and amazing opportunity and honor!

What is at the heart of LuXury Crystal Ireland that you want your customers to take home?

Presenting one-of-a-kind heirloom crystal lighting, tableware, giftware, stemware, barware, and statuary to US and Canadian buyers who gather the light and the stories of hundreds of years of Irish crystal craftsmanship for their own pleasure and for passing on to future generations the beauty and the joy of owning a piece of LuXury Crystal for themselves. It is a privilege.

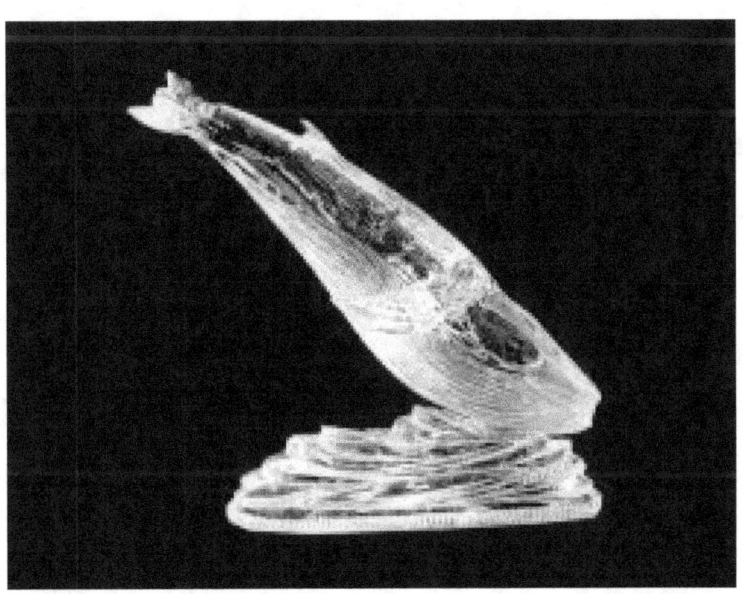

Onna Carr and LuXury Crystal Ireland, can be followed on the platforms listed:

Facebook—https://www.facebook.com/onna.carr.94

LinkedIn—https://www.linkedin.com/in/onna-carr-rddipl-merit-1444a811a/

Websites— http://www.waterfordmadecrystalchandeliers.ie/ and
https://www.thelittlegreenhouseonthecorner.com/luxury-crystal-ireland

YouTube—https://www.youtube.com/watch?v=Mogs0N0r8Ms

All photos courtesy of and used with permission from Noel Finan of LuXury Crystal Ireland.

Friday Finds:

The Interior Designers

Marie Burgos of Marie Burgos Design

May 5, 2017

Marie Burgos with Onna Carr

This week, I am featuring an interview with Marie Burgos of Marie Burgos Design, winner of the Best of Houzz 2017 Service Award. Marie is a native of France, and she got her Masters of Business Management Degree at the University of Paris before continuing her education and receiving a degree in interior design at New York University and her Feng Shui certification through Master James Jay, disciple of Grand Master Lin Yu. Marie specializes in loft and penthouse design, and her work has been featured on HGTV's Unsellables, in Luxury Home Quarterly, and several prestigious, interior design books. Marie has recently released her own product line, which has beautiful as well as functional interior design accents including lighting, art, and furniture.

What led you to start Marie Burgos Design?

In my life, I aspired for more balance, happiness and harmony. Through Feng Shui, I learned that my home environment had a huge influence on my emotions and ultimately, on my achievements and happiness. I have always

admired the architecture and the beauty of Paris, my native country, and with a family who originated from the beautiful island of Martinique, I experienced the color and natural elements of nature in the Caribbean. I also felt that I needed to use my creativity because I am surrounded with creative people in my family. My mother is a painter, one of my brothers is an executive chef, the other is a musician, and my husband, a photographer! For years, I was the only one working in a very corporate career, and the need to use my natural creativity really began kicking in—the rest is history!

What is your favorite aspect of owning and operating your design firm?

One of the strongest aspects of owning your own design firm is the freedom of creating. Living from your art and creativity is for many seen as a dream, but it can be very challenging and very rewarding.

What have you learned the most from opening and running Marie Burgos Design?

The skills that I have learnt from my previous business experience as a general manager have given me the training to run my own firm. Planning, organizing, and customer service are some of the most valuable skills to apply.

What suggestions do you have for others who would like to start a career in interior design?

Be persistent, try new things, and surround yourself with positive people.

What is at the heart of your business that you want your clients to take home?

My approach to creating spaces, which integrates the Feng Shui philosophy, leads me to focus on balance, harmony, the use of natural elements, and the Yin and the Yang forces. These elements are all present in space in the form of a color, texture or shape so that they can bring harmony. Lastly, I apply Yin and Yang. These two opposite forces which create balance together, such as straight lines paired with curves, hard surfaces like a glass table, paired with a plush rug or pillows, dark areas (wall colors or furniture), against a light background or ambient light - it is all about balance and creating a space that looks beautiful but also feels right.

Marie's website, http://www.marieburgosdesign.com, features her work, an informative blog on her projects, an online shop showcasing furniture, curated art, lighting, and accents. Marie Burgos Design can be followed on the platforms listed:

Facebook—https://www.facebook.com/MarieBurgosDesign/

Houzz—http://www.houzz.com/pro/marieburgos/marie-burgos-design

Instagram—https://www.instagram.com/marieburgos.design/

LinkedIn—https://www.linkedin.com/in/manobluedesign

Pinterest—https://www.pinterest.com/MarieBurgosID/

Twitter—https://twitter.com/MarieBurgosID

Photos courtesy of and used with permission from Marie Burgos of Marie Burgos Design

Stephanie Jeffries of The Nista Collection™

June 30, 2017

Stephanie Jeffries with Onna Carr

Headquartered in Coral Gables, Florida, Stephanie is a native of Kettering, Maryland, right outside of the nation's capital and is now completing her Master's of Fine Art in Interior Architecture and Design online at the Academy of Art University in San Francisco after having also attained her Master's of Business Administration in 2010 from the University of Phoenix. As an internationally recognized luxury modern designer, private yacht designer, and online business success coach to other creative professionals, Stephanie's premiere fortes include providing world class photorealistic 3D rendering and opulent design services for both

commercial and residential private investors, ambassadors from abroad, leading professional athletes, entertainers, and C-level executives; particularly as it pertains to ethnic affluence.

What led you to start The Nista Collection™ featuring Designista™ and 3D Rendernista?

Over the last 20 years, my journey as a designer has covered many areas of specialization including custom modern furniture, artwork, rugs, and home fashion design for high-end international retailers and their clients' commercial and residential projects. But, ultimately, the day I stopped limiting seeing myself as only a designer in the conventional sense and embraced myself as more of a creative force that wanted to help other creatives see themselves in the same way, things changed dramatically for me.

Then, the housing crash of 2008 hit our industry particularly hard, it was heartbreaking to see a majority of the incredibly talented designers, architects, stagers, artists, and other tradesmen that I was privileged to know struggle to stay afloat. My own niche was called into question as the Internet changed how we each were able to do business. It shifted much of the exclusivity the trade once had into the hands of consumers. Therefore, maximizing how to monetize oneself as  a designer online was a struggle for many, including myself, until four years ago when I launched The Nista Collection™. Under The Nista Collection™, I have carved out clear segments in highly distinctive divisions for areas I have an insatiable love and proficiency for. This now also features my expertise in providing world class architectural 3D visualizations for luxury real estate developers, construction companies, real estate brokers, private real estate investors, architects, and other designers.

By re-calibrating the approach of my creative business like this, it has made my work and skill set much more unique, marketable, and relevant to the correct crowd of potential customers, both in identifying them and closing more lucrative and fulfilling retainers and contracts. Through impactful 3D rendering, my goal is to provide exceptional three-dimensional photorealistic rendering of a space or place not yet having broken ground on to allow both residential and commercial clients the wonderful emotional experience of seeing their project conceived in a way their senses will best register; more in a 'real life' way we live--in 3D! Renderings also help the pre-sell phase of design and construction become more targeted and cost effective as well. Ambiguity of design intent is alleviated and ensures all interested parties are on the same page. This not only saves money due to lessening the chance of mistakes occurring, but also saves a tremendous amount of time as workflow can be simplified whenever a change does need to be made to conceptual ideas before ordering materials and the first hammer is on the wall or the first shovel goes into the ground. Executed with precision, the visual lines are blurred successfully between an actual photo of a physical space or location and one created using BIM or top-of-the-line CAD software.

What is your favorite aspect of owning and operating your design firm?

 I'm limited only by the restrictions I put on myself in terms of when I want to work and whom I want to work with. I know what it's like to work where you're not entirely in control of your time, the quality or quantity of projects, or clients you work with, and just as important, your income. I also know what that feels like even when you work for yourself. Through all of the ups and downs, backwards and forwards of growing my business, I'm now able to direct my energy in a balanced, holistic way having learned how to automate what I want to be hands-free from, and I have enjoyed showing others how to do the same for several years now. I guess you could say I've become a champion cheerleader for helping develop a multi-millionaire mindset for the creative professional. That part is perhaps the most rewarding of all.

What have you learned the most from opening and running The Nista Collection™ featuring Designista™ and 3D Rendernista™?

Definitely time management, stepping out of my comfort zone, and streamlining my processes through cultivating the right partnerships, relationships, and networks. I value genuine and sincere connectivity, so I'm not a "connection collector." I expect to engage with others by contributing real and dynamic interactions where we can grow and share what we each bring to the table. I've learned to measure my success by how much shorter I can help someone else get to their success by helping them avoid mistakes, pitfalls, and lengthy learning curves that I've gone through myself or have witnessed happen to others.

What suggestions do you have for others who would like to start a career in interior design?

Don't be afraid to be a big fish in a decent-sized pond. Interior designers can end up sounding like we are a dime a dozen by how we describe what we do and how we go about doing it. If there is a particular niche that ignites your pulse like no other when it comes to your creative juices, trust that your gift will not only make room for you in

that specialty, but that you will also lead the pack if you understand how to define who your ideal clients are and what projects you want to work with. From there, marketing yourself becomes more of a natural extension: dare to have the courage to do so with no apologies and I promise you; you will only ever look back to see how far you've come and never to see what you regret.

What is at the heart of your business that you want your customers to take home?

I'll answer this based on consistent feedback that I get from customers and that is that they cherish the individualized approach I commit to each one of them in mapping out both short and long term attainable expectations throughout the design process from consultation to conceptual completion: they are my most treasured point of inspiration. I take pride in meticulously implementing all of the lovely, intimate details customers entrust sharing with me in order for me to deliver a tailor-made mosaic of spaces they'll love to create memories in. Clients rest in my discretion, finesse, and treatment of holding their privacy with a high regard for confidentiality. If they want to have fun, laugh a lot, and be at ease throughout the entire time we work together knowing that their vision is understood by me and will be interpreted with acute accuracy, then I'm the designer and/or 3D renderer for them.

Stephanie's website, http://www.thenistacollection.com/, highlights her business model, market niches, luxury partner network, links to her online portfolio, coaching corner, advertising opportunities, modern inspiration blog, and represents the best way to reach out to her to work with her. You can also reach out to connect with Stephanie, The Nista Collection™, and 3D Rendernista™ can be followed on the platforms listed:

Facebook—https://www.facebook.com/3DRendernista

Instagram—https://www.instagram.com/3DRendernista/

LinkedIn—https://www.linkedin.com/in/stephaniemjeffries/

Pinterest—https://www.pinterest.com/TheNistaCollection/

Twitter—https://twitter.com/NISTACOLLECTION

Photos courtesy of and used with permission from Stephanie Jefffries of The Nista Collection™ featuring Designista™ and 3D Rendernista™

Freelance Interior Designer Kyrsten Attig

August 18, 2017

Kyrsten Attig with Onna Carr

What led you to become an interior designer?

Since I was young, I have always been captivated by design, specifically how the interior and exterior of a building creates a story for the viewer. I enjoyed the idea of creating spaces for people to inhabit—places that inspire certain feelings in people—certain reactions. It really comes down to solving a problem: envisioning and designing an environment to fit the client's needs. I am drawn to the mixture of technical and creative skills as well as the organization and the teamwork needed to pull the entire project together. Like countless people after high school, I had no clue of what I wanted to do. I took 2 years off, dabbling in some courses at a local community college. From this my interest in design grew substantially. I began my journey at Drexel University in Philadelphia, PA, majoring in interior architecture/design. Part of the curriculum included a six-month co-op, where I had the opportunity to pack my bags and to travel to New York, where I worked for Gensler Architects. Through this venture, I was able to learn how the design world actually functions outside of school projects. I was able to work alongside some incredible architects and designers.

Working at such a large firm allowed for tons of opportunity for growth. I was able to create my own path and experience, and I learned a lot about the architectural side of the industry. This eventually led me to my job after graduation, at BLT Architects. BLT has a strong architectural presence in commercial design. I learned and became very adept at the principles of space planning, functionality and construction. At BLT, I gained knowledge and advice from my mentors, which then helped me to branch out on my own for a while. I am currently working from home as a freelance architectural designer, specializing in multi-family housing projects in Brooklyn, New York.

What is your favorite aspect of being an interior designer?

One of my favorite aspects about being a designer is the flexibility within the profession. Architecture and design allow room for an individual to choose their distinctive path. There are various fields of designs to choose from: commercial, residential, education, etc. Within each field come specific requirements—making no two days the same. Some days you may be drafting architectural drawings and other days you may be meeting with clients or on the jobsite.

Along with the industry, we are continuously introduced to new and improved products and designs. Numerous designers become representatives for these companies, acquiring knowledge of each specific detail the products have to offer. Although I must say that my favorite part of interior design is the excitement and fulfillment I sense when the project begins to come together: designing a space that is efficient and eye-catching is crucial.

What have you learned the most from your career in the interior design industry?

Interior design is not all about the creative aspects. Vital factors of design include the knowledge of building structure, codes, space planning, ergonomics, drafting and more. While the job may include picking colors, furniture, and textures, the bulk of the project is drafting, working with architects and engineers, drawing details, etc. When a designer fails in this area details can go very wrong. Learning about the plumbing codes, the electrical, and the load-bearing walls of the structure in question are requirements in order to run a smooth project.

What tips and ideas do you have for others who would like to start a similar career in interior design?

Many individuals think that an interior designer is similar to an interior decorator. This is not the case: interior designers have become very technical. Typically projects run through three stages: schematic design, design development and construction administration. Schematic design is the most creative stage in the process. Designers pick the colors, textures, components and general design. Design development comprises the drafting, architectural details, and how each component fits together. And lastly, construction administration is where the project comes to life. An understanding of local laws and codes are a huge part of the last two phases since updating details and fixing components ensues until the project is actually built.

What is at the heart of your work you want your clients to take home?

We spend so much time in buildings, whether it is your home, your workplace, or a favorite restaurant. With my work, I want to express a vision, and each project can be entirely different in this aspect. My goal is to not only make the client happy, but myself as well. To bring innovative, cost effective and functional design to the table. To leave the client with something they will enjoy for quite some time. This brings fulfillment on my end: knowing that individuals inhabiting the space appreciate it and make it possible.

Kyrsten Attig's portfolio is available at http://kaa788.wixsite.com/ka-portfolio, and she can be followed on the platforms listed:

Facebook—https://www.facebook.com/kyrsten.attig

Instagram: https://www.instagram.com/kyrstenalexisss/

Linkedin—https://www.linkedin.com/in/kyrsten-attig-a302598a/

Pinterest—https://www.pinterest.com/kyrstenalexisss/

Renderings courtesy of and used with permission from Kyrsten Attig.

Kimberly C. Lyons of KCL-IDESIGN, LLC

September 29, 2017

Kimberly C. Lyons with Onna Carr

This week's post features a fascinating in-depth interview with interior designer Kimberly C. Lyons of KCL-IDESIGN, LLC, Kimberly's business and her blog can be visited at http://kcl-idesignllc.com/.

What led you to become an interior designer?

For starters, it would be my obsession for Play-Doh and Crayola Crayons. I was mesmerized and fascinated by the colors—especially the bright ones, such as the lime green and pumpkin orange. With an overly creative mind as a child, I always leaned towards the aesthetics of an object or space. I could feel the power behind color, and I wanted it to be incorporated throughout my surroundings as well as in my life. I strongly felt the need to pull the beauty from objects or from a space. If there was no beauty to be

found, I visualized what could make the object or space come alive. Also, having a profound eye for unique detailing, I became an abstract artist. However, with painting, I was still longing for and missing the love that I felt for spaces. I finally realized that I could have it all if I incorporated painting and design. So, finding beauty through abstract art, objects, and spaces led me to become an interior designer.

What is your favorite aspect of being an interior designer?

My favorite aspect of being an interior designer is being crazy in love with interiors, having a strong obsession for defining the unique aspects and details of all objects within the interior, and

an extraordinary gift for transforming a space into a powerful presence through visualization. The after results are what make me wake up with a super huge smile because I am living each day doing what I was gifted to do—and that is design.

What have you learned the most from your career in interior design?

Understanding what the client envisions for their space(s) is important. As an interior designer, if that means going outside the box and breaking some major design rules, then that is exactly what I will do because I am never afraid to break some design rules! Besides, nothing pleases me more than seeing the face of a smiling client!

What tips and ideas do you have for others who would like to be interior designers?

If you want to become an interior designer, never put your vision for your life on hold. Always believe with strong faith and keep God first. Regardless of where an individual is starting, if the vision is in place and maintained, (in other words, fed with hard work), results will be seen. Always strive to complete each task or goal that has been set, keep pushing through, and I promise the satisfaction of continued endurance will be the reward.

For one to quit is never an option. And I mean never! Make sure that you have a solid foundation and structure, which is education, a true understanding of how to deal with a variety of different clients, a passion for design as if you can not only change an individual's surroundings; but also, their life, and always keep like-minded individuals around for support. Networking is major and can become a great asset in the design industry.

Remember, always stay focused, determined, and keep the creative side alive because, as an interior designer, being creative is one of the most important tools in a designer's belt. Finally, be original: never attempt to walk in anyone else's shoes because you never want to be a copycat. Originality will always hold weight.

What are your favorite features of being an interior designer?

I adore transforming a home where bold colors were not an option to discuss because of not understanding color or because of a feeling of intimidation. As an interior designer, as already stated, I will break a design rule to make sure the client is satisfied. I will tackle a design project that no one else would consider: my reasoning is because there is beauty in everything. With certain spaces, sometimes you are required to be overly creative to pull out the true beauty.

What is at the heart of your career in interior design that you want your clients to take home?

I have a profound love for interior design: my love for interior design surpasses anything that I have ever desired. I always strive to make sure that each design project is perfect from start to finish. I have a unique understanding of interior design that goes hand-in-hand with the finished product (space). My clients are reassured that my creative aspects are coming from a knowledgeable place and that their vision for their home will be a top-priority from start to finish.

Kimberly can be followed on the platforms listed:

Facebook—https://www.facebook.com/KCLIDESIGNLLC/

Instagram—https://www.instagram.com/kclidesign_llc/

LinkedIn—https://www.linkedin.com/in/kimberlyclyons/

Pinterest—https://www.pinterest.com/kclidesignllc

Twitter—https://www.twitter.com/kclidesignllc

All photos courtesy of and used with permission from Kimberly C. Lyons of KCL-IDESIGN, LLC.

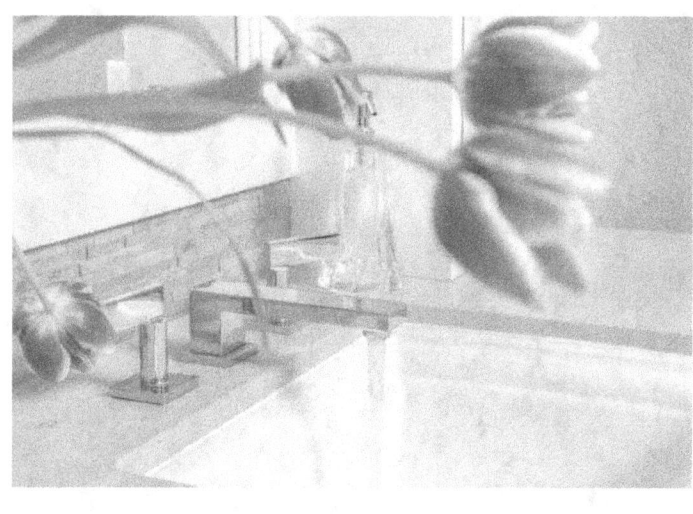

Patti L. Cowger of PLC Interiors

July 21, 2017

Patti L. Cowger with Onna Carr

What led you to PLC Interiors?

I established my first interior design company in 1989 when I was a computer programmer in San Francisco. I was in desperate need of a creative hobby so I met with a few fabric mills and started making table linens. I called my company Tavola Bella ("beautiful table" in Italian). The following year, I took a trip to Italy to visit my grandparents' native home. I was so taken with its artistic and historic beauty that when I came back to the States, I left my programming career and pursued a degree in Architectural Interior Design. I changed my company's name and have been PLC Interiors ever since.

What is your favorite aspect of being an interior designer?

Installation and photo-shoot day. It's when everything I had envisioned, drawn, sourced, and implemented is realized and when clients are the most excited.

What have you learned the most from being an interior designer?

After 28 years, I've learned how to efficiently manage the design process. I've put systems in place that help clients to be more involved (if they choose to be) and I've learned a lot about being a business owner. I've also

learned to trust my instincts and to be bolder in my designs – and that has always paid off. Lastly, I've learned to be sensitive to clients' preferences, values, and goals. I am fortunate and flattered that many of my clients have come back to me over and over through the years. I've been blessed with great relationships, new and old.

What tips and ideas do you have for others who would like to study interior design and create a career out of their passion for interior design?

This will apply to just those who want to own their own interior design business –as opposed to working for an established firm. The passion part of interior design is a must. However, without knowing how to run a business, passion won't matter. It's important to understand who you are, what your brand is, and how you want to conduct your business. Keep a stellar reputation and treat clients the way you'd like to be treated. Get outside help if you can afford it, especially a bookkeeper. Figure out if it makes sense to outsource tasks such as CAD drawings.

What is your favorite project style to work on?

I love to work with fabric and tile, so things like custom bedding and window treatments or bathroom remodels make me really happy.

What is at the heart of your work that you want your clients to take home?

I strongly believe that our environment greatly affects our daily lives. I strive to create functional spaces that make people's lives easier: more organized, less cluttered, and more comfortable. When I can make these spaces beautiful and timeless, as well as a reflection of my clients' personal styles, then I've served them well.

Patti and her interior design company, PLC Interiors can be followed on the platforms listed:

Facebook—http://www.facebook.com/plcinteriors

Pinterest—http://www.pinterest.com/plcinteriors/boards

Website—http://www.plcinteriors.com

Photos 1 and 2 taken by Matt McCourtney Photography, photo3 and 4 taken by Bart Edson Photography, and photo 5 taken by Patti Cowger. All photos used courtesy of and with permission from Patti Cowger of PLC Interiors.

Architect and Interior Designer Jaqueline de Araújo

October 6, 2017

Jaqueline de Araújo with Onna Carr

This week's post features a fascinating and informative interview with Brazilian architect and interior designer Jaqueline de Araújo. Jaqueline is a talented architect and interior designer whose passion for her work and consideration of her clients shines throughout her interview.

What led you to become an architect and interior designer?

My academic degree is architecture and urbanism (urban planning), an area in which I still work. In my architectural projects, especially in the residential projects, I saw the need of my clients to organize the spaces while taking into account the good taste, functionality and a harmonic design. Consequently, a new market opened up for me as a professional interior designer through this process.

What is your favorite aspect of being an architect and interior designer?

My passion for what is beautiful and organization of spaces providing beauty with functionality.

What have you learned from your career in architecture and interior design?

I have learned that we should use psychology, understand our clients, and be able to materialize their dreams and desires. There is no greater satisfaction for an interior designer or an architect than seeing a dream materialized and the client's smile as we deliver a project.

What tips and ideas do you have for others who would like to be architects and/or interior designers?

First of all, the person needs to know if they have a passion for design. Secondly, he or she needs to understand if they have patience in dealing with the potential customer: their cultural differences, lifestyle, and wishes. Thirdly, he or she needs to realize that they have their own a cultural luggage, to understand the arts, and to read and to study—a lot!

What are your favorite features of being an architect/interior designer?

As I mentioned above, the interior designer has to have the ability to materialize the client's desires and needs to have the sensitivity of uniting the beautiful to the functional.

What is at the heart of your career in architecture and interior design that you want your clients to take home?

A good project based on the work of great names, like Mies Van der Rohe (LESS IS MORE) and others. The beautiful, the functional, and the concern in giving the clients what they want in every way—weighing in space as something subjective where the emotions of the human being who will spend their time living or working there are fully considered.

Jaqueline can be followed on the platforms listed:

Facebook— https://www.facebook.com/jaqueline.arquitetaeurbanista

LinkedIn— https://www.linkedin.com/in/jaqueline-de-ara%C3%BAjo-4b620522/

Pinterest—http://www.pinterest.com/plcinteriors/boards

Photo courtesy of and used with permission from Jaqueline de Araújo.

Jacqueline deMontravel, Founder of Ducks Goose

October 20, 2017

Jacqueline deMontravel with Onna Carr

What led you to become an interior designer?

After spending a career in profiling inspiring homes as a magazine editor, where styling a shoot so a room is camera-ready, it was a natural transition.

What is your favorite aspect of being an interior designer?

Meeting people and having an intimate connection to them through their homes. The best way to understand a person is to see how they live, how they cook, what they are proud of, if they allow their kids to drink juice boxes on the couch, and where the pet falls into the family dynamic.

What have you learned the most from your career in interior design?

How design is constantly evolving from a decorate-your-home-once mentality to a perpetual assessment of your home's decor and how your tastes evolve through considering the quickening pulse of home design. Home design has caught up to fashion—now you can update your style every season. Though ordering furniture is not as simple as a new pair of boots, there are simple ways to tweak your spaces though colors, textures, and accents.

What tips and ideas do you have for others who would like to be interior designers?

Connect, connect, connect! If you can't find that special coffee table, work with a craftsman to design one. Want to wallpaper that awkwardly-spaced powder room? Have the best paint and paper specialist on hand to help you navigate such a challenge. You cannot do it all, so build a list of design experts to help you to achieve your goals.

What are your favorite features of being an interior designer?

The long reach of relationships: from clients, to craftsmen, to industry tradesmen who design those amazing products that give a home that wow factor.

What is at the heart of your career in interior design that you want your clients to take home?

For me it's a creative process that is more than strategic placement of pretty objects in a room. It's a mix of the investigative and of psychology with a stylish execution. You must analyze your life and how you want your home to uphold your routine. What colors make you happy? What pieces that can be edited from a room to create an overall balance so all dwellers are in sync?

I also fear that overly-designed look where everything is hotel room perfect—so perfect that an entire room can go into design disarray just because your child didn't leave his backpack in his personalized cubby that could lead to you contributing to a tightly-wound generation. A home's true worth is in its ability to make family and guests feel comfortable. As a stylist and designer, I try to find a balance between real life and style. Personally, I have many beloved things that were either passed down or accumulated on travels that may not fit into today's designer scheme but that are what makes my home interesting and personalized: every belonging has a story that no store-bought accessory can match.

What may be my most valued treasure is my art collection. Since I can remember, my mother educated me in art history as she earned her masters in art and went on to run an art gallery. She would take me to the New York City museums and enlist me to help her analyze the works of art she studied. We traveled often, and those influences are also strong as art was always a part of my lexicon, my homes, and my interests. Now that I am fully educated on the past rock stars of art, such as Rothko, Milton Avery and deKooning, I am interested in today's creators. I still see so many visions inside of me that I have to unleash— in photography, canvas, and mixed media. My greatest design achievement has been to see my works in other people's homes: adding beauty and enhancing their lives.

Jacqueline can be followed on the platforms listed:

Twitter—https://twitter.com/jdemontravel

Instagram—https://www.instagram.com/ducks_goose/

Pinterest—https://www.pinterest.com/jdemontravel

Facebook—https://www.facebook.com/jdemontravel

Photos courtesy of and used with permission from Jacqueline deMontravel.

Founder of Laurence Carr Design Inc.

November 17, 2017

Laurence Carr with Onna Carr

What led you to become an interior designer?

My becoming a designer was influenced by my previous career in the performing arts and fashion in Europe. I have been an artist since birth. My parents often say I used to play musical instruments and sing since I was a toddler. At five years old, I started attending class at a music conservatory school and learned to read music and to play piano. Then, I was introduced to ballet and never stopped dancing for twenty years. I became a professional ballet dancer at the Paris Opera Ballet and later a fashion model. Through all these years, I was embedded in the aesthetics of theatrical costumes, lights and fashion. This is where I learned to put together in magical ways textures, fabrics, furniture, props, and decor with a set of lighting that enhances one's vision. After living on four different continents of the world and having a few different jobs, becoming an interior designer was a natural calling.

What is your favorite aspect of being an interior designer?

The creative part: designing a concept after listening to a client's scope of work and dreams. Also, the final installation phase, when it all comes together after many months of hard work.

What have you learned the most from your career in interior design?

The importance of listening to your client's needs and wishes is invaluable. Exceeding our clients' expectations is what we value most.

What tips and ideas do you have for others who would like to be interior designers?

First, designing must be a passion. Go to school to learn the required drawing and tech skills and see if you are up for the intricate role of an interior designer. To be successful, one has to be detailed-oriented, consistent, a project manager, and have strong visual skills. Always be curious to learn about new products in the architecture and design industry. Learn about art: design, taste, and to appreciate beauty.

What are your favorite features of being an interior designer?

"Less is more" philosophy works in our designed interiors, so it gives room for the following features to stand out: interior architecture, art collections, antiques, noble materials, and rich-textured fabrics and rugs.

What is at the heart of your career in interior design that you want your clients to take home?

My clients take home that I am a soulful designer. I create timeless, life enhanced, happy, and serene spaces that reflect their lifestyle and empower their daily life. I combine excellence in design with mindfulness. In addition, I work with an international perspective. Having lived in many different countries, my creative inspirations are global. My clients enjoy the journey of their interiors' features, which are each so unique.

Laurence can be followed on the platforms listed:

Facebook—https://www.facebook.com/laurencecarrdesign

Houzz—https://www.houzz.com/pro/ltcdesign/laurence-carr-design-inc

Instagram—https://www.instagram.com/laurencecarrdesign/

Pinterest—https://www.pinterest.com/laurencecarrdesign/

Twitter—https://twitter.com/laurencetcarr?lang=en

Website—http://www.laurencecarr.com

YouTube—https://www.youtube.com/c/LaurenceCarr

Photo courtesy of and used with permission from Laurence Carr.

Gilly Craft Interior Designer of Koubou Interiors

November 24, 2017

Gilly Craft with Onna Carr

What led you to become an interior designer?

I had a successful career with British Airways. Circumstances meant that I had to change careers, and so I trained in fashion and design. I started tutoring at the local college and was then asked to tutor in interior design. This meant that I had to do additional qualifications which I did, and, then, I tutored in both subjects for some time. I was being asked to take projects, and it went from there. I had to give up the college as the business was so busy.

What is your favorite aspect of being an interior designer?

Helping clients get the space they want to live or work in.

What have you learned the most from your career in interior design?

Doing research is the most important element of the project. Finding out as much about the client and what they want to achieve is the only way of getting a successful outcome.

What tips and ideas do you have for others who would like to be interior designers?

Do a course or degree depending on how far you want to take your career. Working for a practice and learning how an interior design company works before striking out on your own is also beneficial.

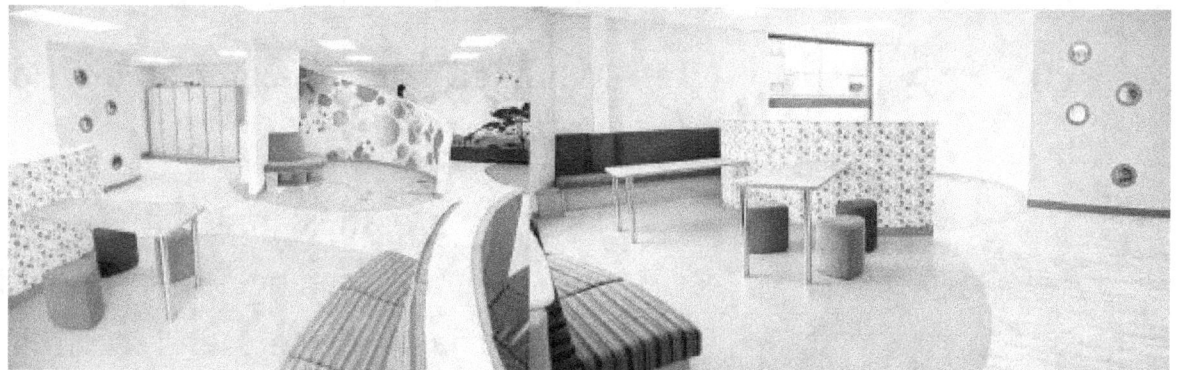

What are your favorite features of being an interior designer?

Always working with interesting people. Being challenged and solving issues. Having an outcome that you can be proud of.

What is at the heart of your career in interior design that you want your clients to take home?

That we care — we recognize that we are spending the client's money, and we want the best outcome within budget.

Photos courtesy of and used with permission from Gilly Craft.

Gilly can be followed on the platforms listed:

Facebook—http://www.facebook.com/koubouinteriors

Instagram—http://www.instagram.com/koubouinteriors

Pinterest—http://www.pinterest.co.uk/koubouinteriors/

Twitter—https://twitter.com/KoubouInteriors

Website—http://www.koubouinteriors.co.uk/

Sara Ho of Sara Ho Designs

December 8, 2017

Sara Ho with Onna Carr

What led you to become an interior designer?

My father is a very talented carpenter and during my childhood he would take me to tour old restored homes in Los Angeles. I fell in love with the beauty of these homes, and the way they transported me to another world when I walked through the door. It wasn't until I became an adult and lost almost everything in hurricane Katrina that I finally started to see interior design as a career. I saw all the devastation around me, the impact that home renovation had on people that needed a fresh start, and I wanted to be part of that. I wanted to help people create beautiful homes: places that were their sanctuaries and places where they felt like they belonged.

What is your favorite aspect of being an interior designer?

I love creating a space for my client that touches on everything they are looking for, plus incorporates elements that they didn't know they wanted or needed. My main goal with every project is to make my client happy and to solve their problems creatively.

What have you learned the most from your career in interior design?

That it's okay to make suggestions to a client contrary to what they ask for. They hire a designer for their expertise, and it's our job to make sure they have thought of everything. It's really fun to see a client get excited about an idea for their space that they never would have thought of. But, I also believe in the old chivalry of business: the client is always right. I am designing for them. I am not for designing for myself or for my reputation.

What tips and ideas do you have for others who would like to be interior designers?

Get a degree. Most people think you can learn it as you go, and you can, but there are so many vital building blocks that you learn in school that are enriched when you are working with your clients. Networking is key in our industry. Go to industry events, get plugged in at your local ASID chapter, and make friends. Vendors are a great resource for designers, so treat them well because your relationship with them will be long lasting. This industry is small when it comes to relationships— always consider your impression on others.

What are your favorite features of being an interior designer?

I love problem solving, designing for function and aesthetics, and seeing a happy client.

What is at the heart of your career in interior design that you want your clients to take home?

Interior design is important. Your surroundings affect your mood and the way you interact with the world around you. In my career, I have designed many spaces: mostly hotel guest rooms, lobbies, clubs, restaurants, and high end residences. The most important aspect of design is how do you feel when you walk into a room. As interior designers, we are experience creators, and the experience is tailored specifically for each client—that is the ultimate goal.

Sarah can be followed on the platforms listed:

Facebook--https://www.facebook.com/sarahodesignsllc/

Instagram--https://www.instagram.com/sarahodesigns/

Pinterest--https://www.pinterest.com/sarahodesign/

Photo courtesy of and used with permission from Sara Ho.

Industrial and Interior Designer, Andrea Gramaccia of Andrea Gramaccia Design

December 22, 2017

Andrea Gramaccia with Onna Carr

What led you to become and interior and industrial designer?

My first approach to industrial design was in 2004, when the designer Andrea Dichiara claimed a course with the support of several companies around our area. In that opportunity, I started to think and to know the real needs of furniture companies and then to understand all aspects of projects as an industrial designer. With interior design, I had the opportunity from the 1st year of high school to educate myself in this field as I learned how understand the fundamentals of interior design and rendering techniques.

What is your favorite aspect of your career in interior and industrial design?

Honestly, there are a lot of aspects and considerations involved in design, but maybe the most important aspect for me is the great possibility to improve or to try to improve the lives and the lifestyles of people. In interior design, it is about the satisfaction and the happiness of customers. If we talk about a space, it is important to insure the people who work and who visit the building feel comfortable and happy to be there. For industrial

design, the purpose is the same, and even if there are different modalities of project, the goal is to make sure that the finished project will be useful to as many people as possible.

What have you learned the most from your career in interior and industrial design?

I am still young in this career, so for now I can only say that even if I love this job, as in many things, there are positive and negative aspects, but they make the process interesting and challenging every day. The most beautiful thing I have learned is: I hope to never say "I have finally learned" because to do this job is the greatest opportunity to learn something and to learn again—every day.

What tips and ideas do you have for others who would like to start a career in interior and industrial design?

I think for first they obviously have to be passionate. Read design magazines; but also, you have to be connected and to pay attention to the fashion, the food, the music, the politics, the economy, the nature and the entire world to 360°. Another very important thing is traveling, which is fundamental to discovery, to being connected, and to being influenced by what you see as when you are in another country or another city you have different perspectives and views come into play. Lastly, listen to everyone and pay attention to elaborate new ideas, concepts, and points of view. When you are able to do all of these things you can be ready to mix all aspects together and to draw your design plans together as a whole from various related parts through a global lens.

What are your favorite features of being an interior designer?

My favorite feature is the possibility to express myself: to provide solutions, to be a hard worker, and to show good taste.

What is at the heart of your career in interior and industrial design that you want your clients to take home?

I want to generate pleasant feelings through my thoughts, my concepts and my projects. The client's voice is the most important part of my work: if I can make their lives happier and more satisfied, and, if after a few years, they still find my solutions good and useful, I don't have anything more to ask—I can be proud of my work.

Andrea can be followed on the platforms listed:

Facebook—www.facebook.com/andreagramacciadesigntry

LinkedIn—www.linkedin.com/in/andrea-gramaccia-56799b55/st

Website—https://www.andreagramacciadesign.com/

All Images courtesy of and used with permission from Andrea Gramaccia.

Interior Designer Davian Rhoads

January 4, 2018

Davian Rhoads with Onna Carr

What led you to start your career in interior design?

Since the early age of seven-years-old, when I found out that I was able to draw and to produce art, I began to expand upon my artistic abilities. I have always been fascinated with the world of art, ranging from paintings, to drawings, to architecture, and to interior design elements. While working for the Army and managing my career as a soldier, I began to realize I needed more from life and a way to connect with people in a more positive light. I knew I wanted to utilize my artistic talents to create enjoyment and to inspire others in life, but I was not sure how to approach this feature.

At one point in my life, I did want to utilize my artistic abilities and go into graphic design. However, I knew the chances of career advancement in that industry was very low because of the nature of the career path.

Once my career in the Army was coming to an end, I ventured out to the beautiful state of Nevada and worked as a security manager for multiple casinos and hotels in the Las Vegas valley. It was not until I became tired of the hustle and bustle of the casino business that I really found my niche for interior architectural design. I noticed that my mind had shifted from the aspects of using my

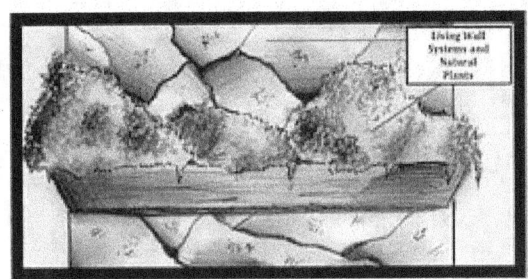

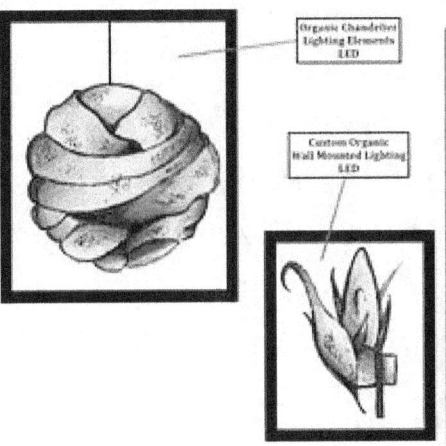

artistic abilities to draw and to create to a more functional feature that utilized these abilities and also allowed me to give back to society and to create designs that were functional, organized, and created a better quality of life and ease for my clients. I also give thanks to the wonderful architecture and interiors I was able to see while living in Las Vegas, which played a major role in developing my interest to create inspiring spaces that spark an emotion or sense within individuals.

I began my interior design journey through the Academy of Art and University out of San Francisco, where I have about a year left until I will have achieved my bachelors degree in interior architectural design. I have had the wonderful opportunity to work for the company, Floor and Décor, where I work as a design manager and create wonderful spaces for individuals. These spaces range from kitchens, to bathrooms, to the interiors of entire homes.

What is your favorite aspect of your career in interior design?

What I find most valuable and my favorite aspect of interior design, is the initial interview with the client(s). This face-to-face meeting with the client(s) sparks the entire flow of creative ideas and design applications that will be used to design and to create the space or the structure. This

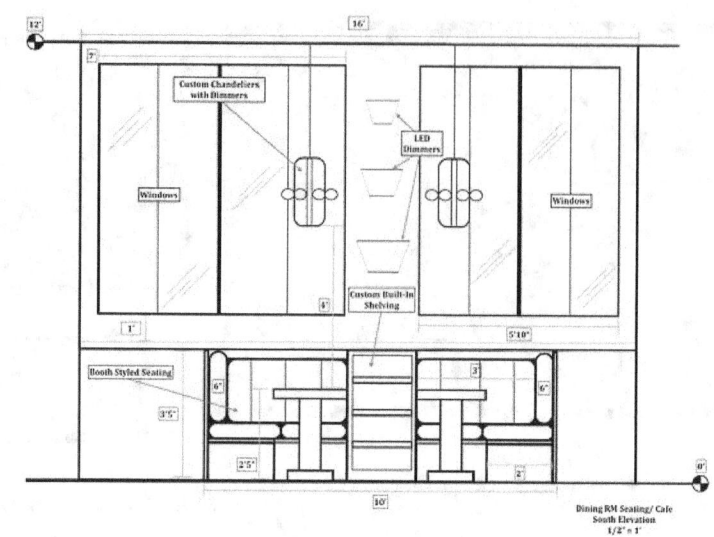

first-hand interview allows me to become acquainted with the client(s) and to develop an understanding of their wants, needs, and even taste within certain design aesthetics and elements. From this initial meeting, I am able to utilize the skill sets I have gained in interior design to bring their visions to life with a mixture of my own taste and styles to create a well-designed and functional space for their enjoyment.

What have you learned the most from your career in interior design?

What I have learned the most from my schooling and interactions with clients is

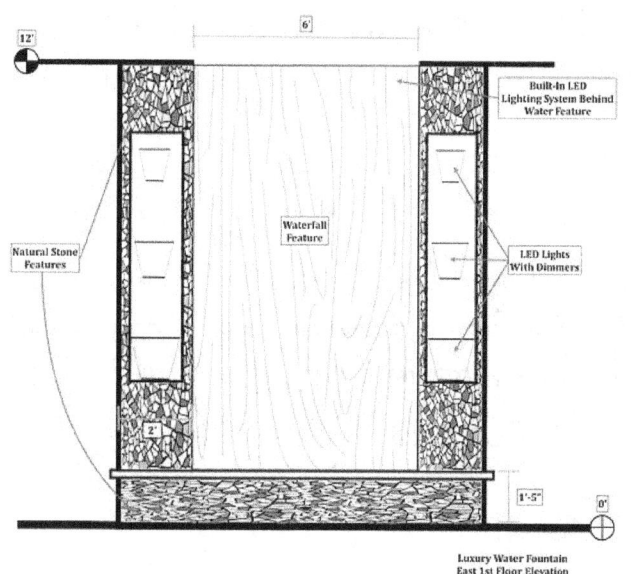

through my current position as a design manager—that every individual client is unique in tastes and has different wants or needs which need to be met in order to feel comfortable within their desired spaces. With this stated, a good designer needs to be able to balance these aspects and to create based on their client's wants and needs. A designer furthermore needs to be able to address certain issues and resolve them for all parties involved to be happy and to move forward with the design process. At the end of the day, the important feature is the client and their views.

What tips and ideas do you have for others who would like to start a career in interior design?

I would have to say keep working hard and developing your skill sets. Secondly, continue to advance your knowledge within the field and ensure you are up to date on the current design trends and capabilities. Without these tools we are not designers, but full time decorators.

What is the favorite aspect of your career in interior design?

I would have to say my favorite aspect of my career is the developing and expressing of ideas through the use of design principles and elements that spark a sense of inspiration and functionality with the design world. The great designer creates spaces that are aesthetically pleasing, but at the same time, remain functional and to create a sense of ease for the users. To make one's life better or to advance their quality of life is the key to design success.

What is at the heart of your career in interior design that you want your clients to take home?

I think that what I want others to take home from my career in interior design is to remember that designing is fun and a challenge at the same time. We are a culture

that is becoming highly advanced and branching out daily within our designs and our quality of life. I think as a population we need to focus more on designs that coexist well with our natural surroundings and to develop ways that utilize natural resources and energies within our designs. We only have one earth to live upon, and I think it's in everyone's best interest to design with her in mind and develop life-cycle structures that embody the use of natural materials and energies incorporated into their designs for a better future.

Davian can be followed on the platforms listed:

Facebook— https://www.facebook.com/Drhoads34

LinkedIn— https://www.linkedin.com/in/drhoads34

Web portfolio—http://drhoads34.wix.com/dr34

All Images courtesy of and used with permission from Davian Rhoads.

Giulia Delpiano Co-founder and Partner of di leG-design

January 12, 2018

Giulia Delpiano with Onna Carr

What led you to become an architect and an interior designer?

At the age of four, I used to pull together a couple of chairs to create the external wall of my "dream house": building a roof with my mom's sheets and making the door and the windows using paper boxes. Then, I brought pillows and cups in to decorate the interior, and I sat on the floor, inside the space that I just created. I already felt like an architect. My parents always say that I learned how to draw and to represent what I wanted to share before talking or walking, but I am sure becoming an architect and interior designer was definitely influenced by looking at my father while he was working at home after dinner— drawing spaces and designing furniture or just talking about technical solutions. He is an engineer. After studying engineering as well, I understood that my path was much more embedded in the aesthetics part of a project, so I studied architecture, and I focused on interior design.

What is your favorite aspect of being an architect and an interior designer?

To support the clients as they define their space: to show them through a mood board and a concept design what they had in mind. "Exactly what I wanted, how did you do that?" is my favorite feedback during the first step of the consultancy. Most of the time, I, as an interior designer, get the features of the design that the client wants way before they realize what they want as I anticipate their needs and their desires. Being surrounded in my daily life by finishes, colors, fabrics and beautiful objects is not a job: it is the dream of that kid who sat down in her house (made of chairs, sheets, and paper boxes) that came true!

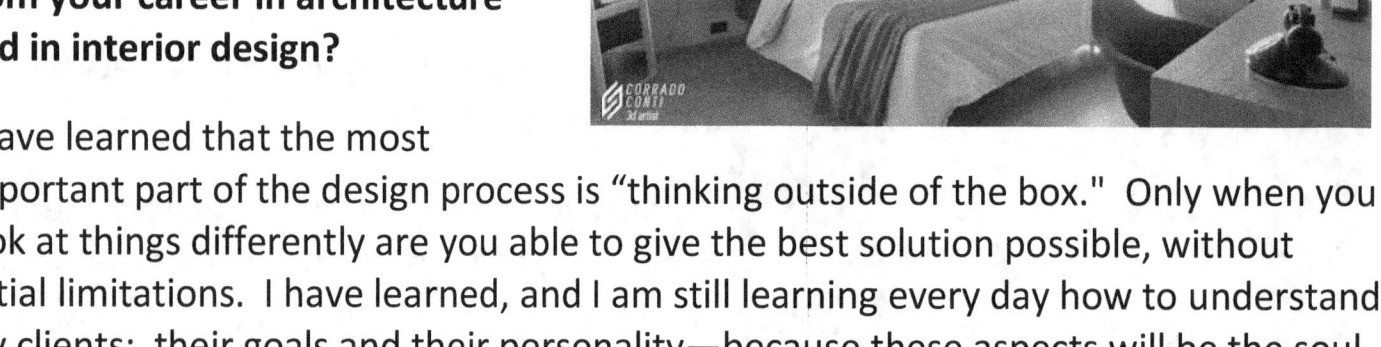

What have you learned the most from your career in architecture and in interior design?

I have learned that the most important part of the design process is "thinking outside of the box." Only when you look at things differently are you able to give the best solution possible, without initial limitations. I have learned, and I am still learning every day how to understand my clients: their goals and their personality—because these aspects will be the soul of their projects.

What tips and ideas do you have for others who would like to be architects and/or interior designers?

If you want to give clients the opportunity to live experiences through the space that you design, you have to live those experiences yourself—a lot—everyday: traveling, reading, knowing yourself deeply, and learning how to listen to others. Being passionate, doing research, studying and then sharing ideas with your team are the most important elements of any project.

What are your favorite features of being an architect and an interior designer?

Being socially and culturally responsive with the opportunity to create something that lasts. One of my favorite features is that I want to be recognizable in my design: always putting something of myself into every project while keeping in mind that the most important parts of any project are representing the clients, their businesses or homes, and their wishes. If I put the representation of myself first, I would be an artist and not an interior designer.

What is at the heart of your career in architecture and in interior design that you want your clients to take home?

That I am not creating just aesthetic but most of all experiences and personal interaction with the interiors that I design: giving people the opportunity to live a moment that they won't forget in a store, a hotel, a restaurant, and in a residential space—making them feel a part of it all is my goal.

Giulia can be followed on the platforms listed below:

Facebook--https://www.facebook.com/giulia.delpiano.3

Instagram—http://www.instagram.com/giuliadelpiano_accent

Pinterest--https://www.pinterest.com/giuliadelpiano/

Websites--http://www.leg-design.com and http://www.giuliadelpiano.com

Images courtesy of and used with permission from Giulia Delpiano.

Shelly Dozier-McKee of ConfettiStyle Interiors

February 16, 2018

Shelly Dozier-McKee with Onna Carr

What led you to become an interior designer, a design and DIY blogger, and a retail consultant?

As a young child, I had a passion for decorating, design and fashion. In addition, I have always been a creative person who loves to craft, to paint, and to make things by hand. My passion for fashion and design led me to study these disciplines in college, where I earned a BA degree in fashion merchandising with a minor in interior design.

After graduating from college, I started my retail career as an assistant buyer for a high-end department store in Seattle and from there moved on to Eddie Bauer, where I advanced to the position of general merchandise manager for catalog and retail, overseeing men's and women's apparel, footwear and non-appeal product categories. During my tenure at Eddie Bauer, I was also fortunate to be involved in domestic and far-east product sourcing, and I traveled to Asia several times a year to work with factories on the production and manufacturing of exclusive products for the company. After 11 years at Eddie Bauer, my husband and I moved to Atlanta, where I became the GMM for a national home decor and gift catalog. I left that position after two-and-a-half years to fulfill a life-long dream of opening my own home decor and gift store.

Within the first few years of business, The Scarlet Tassel was honored with several awards including an ASID Design Excellence Award in 2004, Top 50 National Retail Star award by Home Accents Today in 2005, an ARTS Award finalist nomination in

2005, Best of Atlanta award in 2006, and the Retail Excellence Award for Marketing Achievement by Gifts and Decorative Accessories in 2009. As part of my store portfolio, I also offered residential interior design and holiday decorating services, and I developed a series of seasonal design and lifestyle workshops to educate and to inspire customers on design, decorating, entertaining, and gifting.

What are your favorite aspects of being an interior designer, a design and DIY blogger, and a retail consultant?

While it might seem unusual, education is what I love most about my career as a designer, design blogger, and retail consultant. Yes, I love creating beautiful and functional spaces for clients; but also, I love educating people about design and helping them to discover and to connect with their personal design style.

I started my blog, ConfettiStyle, as a way to share, to educate, and to inspire people through my passion for design, entertaining, gifting, and living a stylish life. The blog is my platform to answer design questions, to help people tackle design challenges, and to inspire them to live their best life with style! My mom was a teacher for 27 years, and it was only a few years ago that I realized that I had her love for educating and uplifting others, just in a different way.

What have you learned the most from your career in interior design, as a design and DIY blogger, and as a retail consultant?

I've learned many lessons throughout my career but none more important that this: surround yourself with people who have dreams, desires, and ambition because they'll help you push for and to realize your own dreams, desires, and ambitions. I'm blessed to have had amazing mentors, business relationships, and friends who inspire

& encourage me through their words, their actions, and by the way they live their lives and go after their dreams.

What are your favorite features of being an interior designer, a design and DIY blogger, and a retail consultant?

As an interior designer, I love the creative process of design—starting with a vision and seeing the vision come to life in a client's home. As a blogger, nothing gives me more joy than to hear from readers how my advice and ideas have impacted their lives in a positive way. As a retail consultant, I love sharing both personal and business lessons that I've learned over the years and knowing that what I share can help someone with the success of their business.

What is at the heart of your career in interior design, in blogging, and in retail consultancy that you want your clients to take home?

Uplifting others is at the heart of everything I do. Inspiring people to find and to follow their passion; helping people to create beautiful homes that bring them joy; and encouraging people to live their joy.

Shelly can be followed on the platforms listed:

Facebook-- https://www.facebook.com/ConfettiStyleInteriors/

Instagram--https://www.instagram.com/confettistyle/

Pinterest--https://www.pinterest.com/ConfettiStyle/

Twitter--https://twitter.com/confettistyle

Website/Blog--http://confettistyle.com/

All photos courtesy of and used with permission from Shelly Dozier-McKee of ConfettiStyle Interiors.

Interview with Dina Caruso: Hospitality Design Consultant

March 16, 2018

Dina Caruso with Onna Carr

What led you to become an interior designer?

Here is the honest, non-flowery answer: as a college student, I did not know what I wanted to study. I started in psychology, and then changed to marketing, and I started to pursue a minor in business. Perplexed, I pulled out my 7th grade aptitude test and saw "interior design" as a top career choice for me. I called to tell my mother and she said "Well . . . you were always good at rearranging your room and creating a lot of different outfits out of very few clothes so maybe interior design or fashion design is the answer." Since I lived in sweatpants and baseball hats at that stage of my life, fashion was not the answer. Hence, I chose interior design. Little did I know that interior design would be a career requiring some knowledge of psychology, marketing and business. God knew what he was doing. I wasn't flailing, I was preparing!

What is your favorite aspect of being an interior designer?

I love having the ability to create "feel good" environments. We can influence mood and behavior via interior design. We can use our talents and skills to truly help people feel a certain way.

What have you learned the most from your career in interior design?

I have learned how to work in a team, how to work solo, how to work quickly, how to focus, how to manage time, how to communicate with people from different cultures and socio-economic conditions, the list is endless. The best learning experiences have come from the travel portion of the job.

What tips and ideas do you have for others who would like to be interior designers?

Take the time to learn the business aspects of the profession sooner rather than later. It will help whether you decide to work for yourself or for someone else. If you are interested in any type of commercial design (hospitality, healthcare, office buildings, etc.), enroll in an accredited program at a school where you will learn the necessary software skills.

What are your favorite features of being an interior designer?

My favorite perks are meeting people, traveling to new places, seeing new things.

Dina can be followed on the platforms listed:

Instagram--https://www.instagram.com/dinapcaruso/

Pinterest--https://it.pinterest.com/dinapcaruso/

Images courtesy of and used with permission from Dina Caruso.

Interview with Interior Designer, Diana Deitrick

March 23, 2018

Diana Deitrick with Onna Carr

What led you to become an interior designer?

I was artistic as a child, I loved to build models, draw, take pictures and I would wonder at architecture. In high school, I attended an interior design career workshop by FIDM, and, after the workshop, I knew that interior design was how I wanted to express my creativity. I liked the idea that every project would be different: a different set of challenges, different people, and different sites.

What is your favorite aspect of being an interior designer?

The conceptual phase: the part where I get to come up with ideas, the concept, the theme, the vibe of the space. I love to the or go to the site and study it, then visualize the space according to what I see with its limits and challenges.

What have you learned the most from your career in interior design?

How to listen to the client, the team, and the end-user. It is important to understand what the objective and end result needs to be.

What tips and ideas do you have for others who would like to be interior designers?

Learn the small details, learn how things work, be resourceful, keep learning and push yourself to create out of your comfort zone: that's how you learn your style—your niche.

What are your favorite features of being an interior designer?

My favorite thing about being an interior designer is being able to help people thrive

in their space and being able to meet wonderful clients who become long-term friends. In terms of the daily duties of being an interior designer, I love the research part: sourcing materials, coming up with the theme— the concept.

What is at the heart of your career in interior design that you want your clients to take home?

I want my clients to experience the space in a way that they feel inspired, motivated, energized, and relaxed: a place that improves their quality of life.

Diana can be followed on the platforms listed:

Instagram--https://www.instagram.com/dideitrick/?hl=en (and, in the near future, allthingsinteriordesign)

Pinterest--https://www.pinterest.com/deitrickdesigns

Website--http://www.ddintdesign.com

Photo 1 courtesy of Neonbrand on Unsplash, photo 2 courtesy of Joshua Ness on Unsplash, and photo 3 courtesy of Jason Briscoe on Unsplash.

Sim Barker, Color Specialist, Interior Design Lecturer, and Interiors Writer

March 30, 2018

Sim Barker with Onna Carr

What led you to become a color specialist, an interior design lecturer, and an interiors writer?

My work with color started as a result of working for a designer paint company: Mylands. I teach interior design because I love having the opportunity to communicate design ideas and to encourage students to grow creatively.

What is your favorite aspect of being a color specialist, an interior design lecturer, and interiors writer?

Having the chance to curate color collections is a great privilege.

What have you learned the most from your career as a color specialist, as an interior design lecturer, and as an interiors writer? My students teach me a lot about humanity: our wants and needs, how we can make the best of what we have, and how we can sometimes un-knowingly stifle our own creativity.

What tips and ideas do you have for others who would like to be color specialists, interior design lecturers, and interiors writers?

I would always go to art school to get a good grounding before making a decision on which direction you want to go in.

What are your favorite features of being a color specialist, an interior design lecturer, and an interiors writer?

I love working with the color schemes I create in client homes. Color works like alchemy and can totally change a space: refreshing preconceived ideas and even making our older stuff look new!

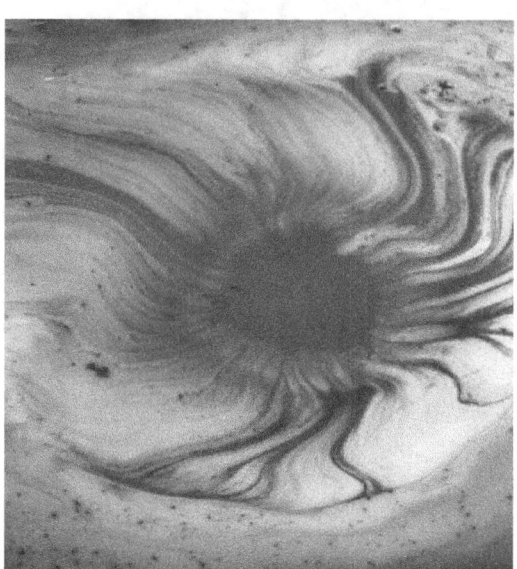

What is at the heart of your career as a color specialist, as an interior design lecturer, and as an interiors writer that you want your clients, students, and readers to take home?

I would like all of us to do two things:

1. Remember that the whole family needs to be involved in color choices for the home.
2. Decorate for the people who live in the home—not the people who visit.

Sim Barker can be reached via the following platforms:

Blog—https://simbarker.wordpress.com/

Website—http://www.simbarker.com/

Photo 1 courtesy of Sharon Pittaway on Unsplash, photo 2 courtesy of Ronald Cunyon on Unsplash, and photo 3 courtesy of Joel Felipe on Unsplash.

Interior Designer, Paddy Rasmussen of New Beginnings

September 3, 2018

Paddy Rasmussen with Onna Carr

What led you to start New Beginnings?

As a result of my own grief and having gone through all three of my avatars: the loss of a loved one, a divorce, and downsizing. I started the planning stages in July of 2016.

What is your favorite aspect of New Beginnings?

That I get to help people transition by providing essential and supportive services.

What have you learned the most from New Beginnings?

That everybody is at different stages of transition.

What tips and ideas do you have for others who would like to start an interior design business?

Figure out what you are most passionate about, put a plan together, and give it your all!

What is at the heart of New Beginnings that you want your clients to take home?

We are here to walk with you as you embrace change and adapt to a new environment. Our core philosophy is to be compassionate and empathetic while providing much needed strength and guidance to help you move forward so you can fully engage in life again.

Meredith Clements of Hamford Interiors

September 10, 2018

Meredith Clements with Onna Carr

What led you to become an interior designer?

Although I've always loved art and design, I never originally wanted to go down that route as a career. When I was a little girl, I wanted to work with animals because I loved them. As I got older, I decided I wanted to pursue a medical career instead, specifically cardiology consultancy. Upon taking my A Levels in Sixthform, a medical career started to appeal less and less to me. I began to think a lot about what I really wanted to do in life--what I'd thoroughly enjoy doing for the rest of my life and realized it was definitely something creative. I left Sixthform at the age of 17, and I tried my hand at freelance Interior Design, much to the horror of clients when I'd walk in to their homes to assess a potential job practically still a child! It was a success, despite my age often making clients apprehensive, and I set up a company specializing in residential Interior Design.

What is your favorite aspect of being an interior designer?

I think there are many different aspects to my being an interior designer that make it thoroughly enjoyable, but the best is definitely seeing the job completed and having everything: the color scheme, the textures, and the surfaces coming together in harmony. I love seeing the client happy with the end result too!

What have you learned most from interior design?

I think what being an interior designer taught me is that, fundamentally, you should always pursue what makes you happy in life. I'm so grateful to be in a career that I thoroughly enjoy. Life is definitely not to be wasted being unhappy overworking yourself in a job you dislike. This I cannot stress enough.

What tips and ideas do you have for others who would like to be interior designers?

 Find your signature style and color; mine is a mixture of traditional & contemporary. The colors I favor working with are neutrals with soft undertones as anything with a heavy undertone tends to date quickly. You want your designs to be timeless and opulent--not to look outdated after a year!

What is your favorite aspect of interior design?

Definitely the getting to work with different styles of furniture and fabrics: they're all so stunning and encapsulating! Whether it is fine silks from Italy or dated leather—each has its own beauty.

What is at the heart of your interior design that you want your clients to take home?

I think it's paramount that your home is a place where you can find solace and comfort. The design of a space has a direct impact on our happiness and the way we feel overall. It's extremely important that a home should be a reflection of the people who live in it. Our homes should hold a certain presence that is both beautiful and encapsulating that incites happiness and joy in all who see them. This is what I always strive to achieve.

Photos courtesy of Meredith Clements of Hamford Interiors.

Meredith can be followed via the following platforms:

Facebook—https://www.facebook.com/HamfordInteriors/

LinkedIn—https://www.linkedin.com/in/meredith-c-5b2b7099/

Instagram—https://www.instagram.com/meredithclements_/

Twitter—https://twitter.com/MClements1?lang=en

Nancy Iraggi of nki|design

November 12, 2018

Nancy Iraggi with Onna Carr

This Week's Friday Finds features Nancy Iraggi, interior designer of nki|design, an interior|exterior Design firm out of Los Angeles and Dallas specializing in space planning, interior architecture and hardscape design through a thoughtful bespoke service.

What led you to become an interior designer?

Where to begin! So many roads all converged at once and threw me into my destiny. My father was a businessman who would redesign our home on the weekends, my mother right by his side, transforming flea market finds for the new areas . . . a family affair really.

My 12th summer was spent as an exchange student in Mexico City, this exotic eye-opening experience marked the precise moment I became visually aware. This was followed by art school, visual display design (windows and retail store design), and surface design. My Interior Design career began with a foray into retail with a "green" eco-home furnishings boutique in Dallas' Deep Ellum Arts District in the early nineties. It was called "Eco-Fluence Studios," and I like to think of it as the very first "Anthropologie." We created a lifestyle brand that sold vintage textiles, toasters, and furniture and were the first to carry aroma therapy diffusers and oils. We also led workshops on Saturday mornings in our studio for various decorative arts subjects such as flower pressing and mono-print making.

THIS PAGE: A Regency console graces the inviting entryway.

What is your favorite aspect of being an interior designer?

My favorite aspect is space planning to enhance interior design's function. I enjoy the palpable feeling of balance that comes from a well-planned space. I also appreciate the interview/discovery process between the client and myself. The reciprocal action that occurs as we discuss the design needs and lifestyle considerations and the mutual trust that is derived from that interaction is enjoyed.

What have you learned the most from your career in interior design?

That listening is the most important tool we have as designers and that most people have trouble editing their possessions because of an emotional attachment.

What tips and ideas do you have for others who would like to be interior designers?

Just do it! Start building a portfolio using spaces you have designed for yourself, friends or relatives. If you haven't designed any spaces yet, create designs for spaces. Practice and develop your skill set. Your hand renderings, CAD plans, and elevations convey your vision to your clients and future employers.

Lastly, I have learned to be mindful of personal boundaries and respectful of others' personal tastes and cherished possessions. Kindness and understanding go a long way into easing a client into changes that may be difficult for them.

What are your favorite features of being an interior designer?

I really love the bones of the house. Improving upon and redesigning the interior architecture to visually enhance and improve the flow and balance of the space. Right along with that would be the material selection and fabrication. Last, but certainly not least, would be lighting.

What is at the heart of your career in interior design that you want your clients to take home?

I would have to say the value. So many people think that interior design is for the very wealthy and without merit--just about making something visually attractive. But the strength of interior design lies in its capacity to be life changing, facilitating day-to-day activities, and enhancing the things that people love about their lives. Most importantly, the joy that is manifested from the changes in people's environments is at the heart of nki|design.

Nancy can be followed on the platforms listed:

Twitter: https://twitter.com/nancyiraggi?lang=en

Instagram:

https://www.instagram.com/nancyiraggi/and https://www.instagram.com/nancyiraggidesigns/

Pinterest: https://www.pinterest.com/niraggi/

Facebook: https://www.facebook.com/niraggi?ref=br_rs

Emmy Award-Winning Set Designer, Jennifer Herwitt

November 21, 2018

Jennifer Herwitt with Onna Carr

What led you to your career as a set decorator?

I have always wanted to work in the film industry since I can remember. I went to Los Angeles on my own at the age of 16 and forged my career. I started in commercials: in the 80's commercials were a booming industry. From there, I moved into music videos working with some of the world's most popular artists including Madonna.   I moved on to film before I went on to sitcoms like The Norm Show and then one-hour dramas! I have been truly blessed to work with some of the greatest directors, actors, and crews! Working on CSI Las Vegas was ideal. Grissom, played by William Peterson, was an entomologist! His office was fun for me to spread my wings with design, my love of insects, and cutting-edge technology that the world had not known before. Our show not only changed the face of television and state of the art technology: it helped forge the path for forensic technology.

What is your favorite aspect of your career as a set decorator?

Getting the opportunity to create a silent character of who that person is, how they live, what their life looks like. Working with the actors to help develop and create a real understanding of who their character is a rare privilege. How they think, what they are interested in, how they live—I get to

experience and to create endless worlds and environments and to step into other people's experiences.

What have you learned the most from your career as a set decorator?

I love to create environments for all walks of life: it's fascinating to me. I feel honored to support the most talented Directors, DP's, and work with the world's best actors.

What tips and ideas do you have for others who would like to start a career in set decorating?

Do IT!

What are your favorite features of set decoration?

The art history: the different time periods and what and how they affected every aspect of how people lived during those times. That beyond all expectations, I was blessed to be nominated for 4 Emmys and actual won two! Not in my wildest dreams could I have imagined that for my life. I am truly humbled for being recognized. I am honored to be associated with that caliber of professionals for something I consider a labor of love!

What is at the heart of your career in set decoration that you want those who see your projects to take home?

How much detail and time goes into developing a set and a character.

Jennifer can be followed on the platforms listed:

Etsy—https://www.etsy.com/shop/JHerwittLivingJewels

Facebook—https://www.facebook.com/herwitt

Facebook Page—https://www.facebook.com/JHerwitt-304095069626047/ and https://www.facebook.com/Jherwitt/

Instagram—https://www.instagram.com/jherwitt_jewels/?hl=en and https://www.instagram.com/jenniferherwitt/?hl=en

Jewelstreet—https://www.jewelstreet.com/collections/Jherwitt

LinkedIn—https://www.linkedin.com/in/jennifer-herwitt-15a819b/

Lyst—https://www.lyst.com/designer/jherwitt/

Moddlinc—http://moddlinc.com/jennifer-herwitt/

Pink Lion—https://www.pinklion.com/shops/365-jherwitt

Pinterest— https://www.pinterest.com/jherwitt/ and https://www.pinterest.com/jherwittjewelry/?eq=J%20herwitt&etslf=20370

Twitter—https://twitter.com/JHerwittJewelry

Friday Finds:

The Foodies

Heather Chase of http://www.theculinarychase.com

July 7, 2017

By Heather Chase with Onna Carr

This Week's Friday Finds features Heather Chase http://www.theculinarychase.com in a delicious interview on her unique website that features her foodie experiences in New York, Hong Kong, Singapore, and Bangkok.

What led you to start http://www.theculinarychase.com?

I was living in Hong Kong, and I had just come back from a trip to Nova Scotia, Canada. I was inspired by the foodie culture there, and I wanted to write about it but I was unsure what form that would be. A friend of mine said I should start a food blog. That was in 2006, and back then food blogs were just getting started. I had no idea at the time what a food blog was but I sleuthed the internet for ideas.

I love the name of your website, and I am just curious how you arrived at "http://www.theculinarychase.com**" for a name?**

My husband said my food blog should incorporate my surname and he coined the name "The Culinary Chase" while we were in a coffee shop in Hong Kong. My blog went live in August 2006.

What is your favorite aspect of managing http://www.theculinarychase.com?

Freedom to write and photograph what I love doing— cooking.

What have you learned the most from http://www.theculinarychase.com?

I'm a self-taught cook, and I initially I wanted to blog about food and the health benefits derived from it. But, as I posted, I noticed people really liked the "how to" posts: simple, everyday tasks in the kitchen that I take for granted and assume everyone knows how to do. I try to keep my posts simple, easy to make, and I always share a tip or two.

What tips and ideas do you have for others who would like to start a similar, food-centered website?

Do what makes you smile. It will come through in every post you write and make sure you have good photos. Everyone likes a story.

What is your favorite feature of http://www.theculinarychase.com?

Gosh, there are so many over the years. I think my style has evolved from the early days, and I didn't really get my photography skills up to snuff until 5 years ago. I still struggle with photography sometimes as I am shooting as it comes out of the oven or off the stove. My husband is patient when I tell him I'm going to take photos of the food before we eat.

What is at the heart of http://www.theculinarychase.com that you want your visitors to take home?

What I answered in the question regarding tips and ideas for those who want to start a food blog: do what makes you smile. It will come through in every post you write and make sure you have good photos. Everyone likes a story.

Heather Chase and her website, http://www.theculinarychase.com, can be followed on:

Instagram—https://www.instagram.com/theculinarychase/

Pinterest—https://www.pinterest.com/heatherchase/

Twitter—https://twitter. com/culinarychase

Photo 1 courtesy of Heather Chase and photo 2 courtesy of Brook Lark on Unsplash.

Debbie Fred of Paleo Eats

July 28, 2017

Debbie Fred with Onna Carr

Paleo Eats founder and CEO, Debbie Fred, is interviewed this week on Friday Finds. Debbie's company, Paleo Eats, creates paleo bars in three varieties: Chai Spice, Coconut Cacao Bar, and Coffee Bean. Paleo Eats' bars can be purchased ($48 for 12 bars) or via a subscription service at their website, http://www.paleoeats.com.

What led you to start Paleo Eats?

I started Paleo Eats in 2012. I had always loved baking, and when each of my 3 children showed symptoms of food intolerances, I had to learn an entirely new way of baking without gluten, dairy or grains. This new way of baking and self-education turned into a business! I had never envisioned myself as an entrepreneur, but here I am, and I'm so happy I am!

I love the name of your business, and I am just curious how you arrived at "Paleo Eats" for a name?

Thank you! You know, I had no rhyme or reason! I had a business partner at the time, and we came up with this name together. We wanted it to be super obvious that this is "Paleo," and that "Paleo" was important to us.

What is your favorite aspect of owning and operating Paleo Eats?

I am very passionate about education. I've had too many people around me suffer from autoimmune diseases, etc. and prevention is key. There are way too many people nowadays being diagnosed with celiac disease or some sort of food-related disease. I'm not just out there selling bars. I want people to know why it's important to eat this way: super clean.

What have you learned the most from opening and running your business?

Oh my—I'm constantly learning! Being in business by myself, there are a lot of hats I must wear. I'm always listening to podcasts, reading books and articles—I've learned what I'm good at and what I need to allocate. I've learned I'm not as organized as I seem!

What tips and ideas do you have for others who would like to sell specialty food products?

I have received SO much guidance here in Bend. There are so many food entrepreneurs here and business groups to join; it's been a wonderful ride. I would just say to go out there and to ask for help. Talk to business owners who you look up to: they're all willing to help you out. I know I'm always willing to pass on the information I've

learned. We should all want each other to succeed!

What is at the heart of your business that you want your customers to take home?

I want them to know that I am a mother of 3 kids, ages 6, 8 and 10. My passion for this business all stemmed from my children. I'm all about PREVENTION. So many diseases stem from inflammation. If we cut down on those inflammatory foods that we put in our body, our chances of staying healthy and leading an active life are so much greater.

Debbie Fred and her business, Paleo Eats, can be followed on the following platforms:

Facebook: https://www.facebook.com/Paleo-Eats-245332042229057/

Google+: https://plus.google.com/+Paleoeats

Instagram: https://www.instagram.com/paleoeatsenergybar/

Pinterest: https://www.pinterest.com/paleoeats/

Twitter: https://twitter.com/PaleoBend

YouTube: https://www.youtube.com/c/paleoeats

Photos courtesy of and used with permission from Debbie Fred of Paleo Eats.

Karista Bennett: Professional Recipe Developer, Photographer, and On-air Talent

January 19, 2018

Karista Bennett with Onna Carr

What led you to become a professional recipe developer, photographer, and on-air talent?

Once upon a time I couldn't cook. I always said anything I cooked could have caused a slow and painful death, which is why I ended up in culinary school in 1999. I had been on hiatus from my first career in healthcare, and I decided to take the plunge into the culinary world. After culinary school, I found myself working as a food writer, caterer, prep chef, cheese specialist, culinary instructor, sous chef, and I ultimately started my own private chef company in 2009. In 2013, I had the privilege of traveling to Italy with a California winery to learn about how they made their Italian Chianti's. I was asked by the winery if I would develop recipes to pair with their wine: that was the beginning of my career as a professional recipe developer. Once I realized how much I loved developing and photographing recipes, I decided to take a bit of a turn and focus on food writing and publishing. I approached several food and lifestyle publications about developing recipes and photographs for them, and the rest is history. It just snowballed from there – leading to requests for on-air recipe demos as well as brand work and online publishing.

What is your favorite aspect of being a professional recipe developer, photographer, and on-air talent?

Sharing my knowledge, experience and talent. I feel so lucky I get a chance to do what I love, and I feel even luckier that I get to share it with others. Sharing my recipes and photographs is extremely personal for me. Food is the element that brings us to the table, where memories are made and life is lived. To be able to bring families and friends together over an enchanting meal makes the hard work worth every moment.

What have you learned the most from your career in professional recipe development, photography, and on-air talent?

This business is hard work. It's fickle; it's in a constant state of change; it's extremely competitive; it's sometimes cruel; and it's not always fair. There are times I have to block out all the noise and be true to myself and to my mission. I've learned that I must be authentic, have confidence in my talent, trust my gut, and then the good stuff will follow.

What tips and ideas do you have for others who would like to be professional recipe developers, photographers, and on-air talents?

Practice, practice, practice. Although I had the good fortune to attend culinary school (and that is a very good thing for me), many professional recipe developers and food photographers have not gone to culinary school. And that's ok! However, they've worked in the culinary world in one capacity or another and practiced their craft. Build your knowledge and experience by attending classes in cooking, writing, photography and stage performance. Or better yet, get a job cooking at a local café or restaurant. Research and never stop learning, be open to change and to new ideas, ask lots of questions and seriously practice every chance you get. Don't be afraid to ask others in this business for advice: there are many of us out there that are willing to help you succeed. In addition, a really awesome web developer and knowledge of SEO is also very helpful.

What are your favorite features of being a professional recipe developer, a photographer, and an on-air talent?

Can you believe I love to cook! (wink wink). For me, it's a thrilling exercise to create new recipes that tantalize the taste buds and excite the food soul. Creating the recipe is always exciting, but getting the perfect "shot" that interprets the recipe perfectly is the most thrilling. I call it getting the "money shot." I think demonstrating recipes on-air has been an interesting component of my career. It seemed a natural extension of what I do and has been a huge learning experience—one that I feel has made me a more confident culinary professional.

What is at the heart of your career in professional recipe development, photography, and on-air talent?

My mission is to connect and inspire: visually through my photos and physically through taste as people try my recipes. Food should not only satisfy hunger, it should feed the soul, nourish the body, and delight the senses. Food is often comfort, joy, healing and sometimes, spiritual. The act of cooking or feeding people gives me a deep sense of joy: it feels as if this is what I was always meant to do.

Karista can be followed on the social media platforms listed below:

Blog--http://www.karistaskitchen.com

Facebook--http://www.facebook.com/karistaskitchen

Instagram--http://www.instagram.com/lifearoundmytable

Pinterest--http://www.pinterest.com/karistaskitchen

Twitter-- http://www.twitter.com/karistaskitchen

Website--http://karistabennett.com

Photos courtesy of and used with permission from Karista Bennett.

Karie Engels of Basil and Salt Magazine

February 23, 2018

Karie Engels with Onna Carr

What led you to start Basil and Salt magazine?

I began Your Home with Karie Engels with a Facebook page and foodie site about seven years ago. At some point I realized that the look of the site and content placed there needed a "refresh" button. I played around the different styles and themes, but I was unable to achieve the depth I was looking for.

While searching for advertising and venues for another project on my board, it just clicked. If I took my site to print, I could create layers, a plethora of voices and fresh, seasonal content while at the same time creating an advertising venue for other projects. I removed my name from the title, and *Basil & Salt Magazine* was born.

What is your favorite aspect Basil and Salt magazine?

Unlimited creativity. There isn't a template, there isn't a specific formula that I am required to follow, which means whatever is happening in the world, however things change in the food or lifestyle industry, we can keep up with news in real-time. I give my contributors the same creative license. I may have a general outline of what I am looking for, yet I trust their instincts. They work in this industry and have their fingers on the pulse of everything that's current. I can add content or remove content in the very last moments before it goes live, and if necessary, again before it goes to print.

What have you learned the most from Basil and Salt magazine?

A huge smile crossed my face as I read the above question. I am still learning the publishing business, and I will continue to soak in knowledge. Every. Single. Day. I jumped into the deep end and was way over my head in an incredibly exciting way. If I could rethink the process and do it all over again, would I? Oh yes, definitely.

What tips and ideas do you have for others who would like to start a culinary magazine?

If it's in your soul to do this, do it. Be creative and stay true to your message. Don't compare yourself to other publications—try and set yourself apart from them. Most importantly, don't be afraid to stray off course a bit if your instincts tell you to go in a slightly different direction.

What is at the heart of Basil and Salt magazine that you want your readers to take home?

Enjoy life. Live it out loud.

Karie and Basil and Salt magazine can be followed on the following social media platforms:

Facebook—https://www.facebook.com/homewithkarieengels/

Instagram—https://www.instagram.com/basilandsalt/

LinkedIn— https://www.linkedin.com/in/karie-engels-8385341a/

Photos 1 and 2 courtesy of Brook Lark on Unsplash.

www.ingramcontent.com/pod-product-compliance
Lightning Source LLC
Chambersburg PA
CBHW082008230526
45468CB00023B/2708